Double Standard

PRAISE FOR *DOUBLE STANDARD*

"In this closely argued, detailed, and meticulous book, James W. Russell compares the development of social policies in the United States and in European states, pointing out areas where there are significant differences of approach but also those where one has borrowed from another. The strong historical and philosophical basis for Russell's analysis continues to make this a novel, engaging, and challenging addition to the comparative literature and an important source book for scholars of the U.S. welfare system." —**Gary Craig**, professor emeritus, University of Hull, United Kingdom

"*Double Standard* is accessible, responsible, historically minded, and classically informed comparative social policy and political sociology. One can only hope others take Russell's example of how to write and do the social sciences. While capturing nuanced differences among European countries, this updated *Double Standard* shows students and scholars the main areas of difference between European approaches to social inclusion and American individualism." —**Robert J. S. Ross**, Clark University

PRAISE FOR THE FIRST EDITION

"James Russell restores my faith in sociology as the best line of inquiry into nagging political questions that too often get assigned to narrow-minded economists. We need books like this to combat academic provincialism as much as to correct social inequality." —**John R. MacArthur**, publisher of *Harper's Magazine* and author of *The Selling of Free Trade*

Double Standard

Social Policy in Europe and the United States

Second Edition

James W. Russell

ROWMAN & LITTLEFIELD PUBLISHERS, INC.
Lanham • Boulder • New York • Toronto • Plymouth, UK

Published by Rowman & Littlefield Publishers, Inc.
A wholly owned subsidiary of The Rowman & Littlefield Publishing Group, Inc.
4501 Forbes Boulevard, Suite 200, Lanham, Maryland 20706
http://www.rowmanlittlefield.com

Estover Road, Plymouth PL6 7PY, United Kingdom

British Library Cataloguing in Publication Information Available

Library of Congress Cataloging-in-Publication Data

Russell, James W., 1944–
   Double standard : social policy in Europe and the United States / James W.
Russell.—2nd ed.
      p. cm.
   Includes bibliographical references and index.
   ISBN 978-1-4422-0657-1 (cloth : alk. paper)—ISBN 978-1-4422-0658-8 (pbk. : alk.
paper)— ISBN 978-1-4422-0659-5 (electronic)
   1. Social policy—Comparative method. 2. Europe—Social policy. 3. United
States—Social policy. 4. Social policy—History. I. Title.
   HN28.R87 2011
   320.6094—dc22
                                                                        2010021238

∞ ™ The paper used in this publication meets the minimum requirements of
American National Standard for Information Sciences—Permanence of Paper for
Printed Library Materials, ANSI/NISO Z39.48-1992.

Printed in the United States of America

Contents

Note to the
Second Edition

The first edition came out in late 2006, before the 2008 presidential campaign in the United States, the beginning of the Great Recession, and the passage of health reform. All three bore on the central theses and concerns of the book.

European social versus American free-market capitalism emerged as a background theme of the presidential campaign. Republicans accused the Democrats of having a socialist agenda, by which they meant adopting European-style reforms. Hedzig Herzman, writing in the *New Yorker*, captured the Republican insinuations: "The dystopia [John McCain] abhors is not some North Korean–style totalitarian ant heap but, rather, the gentle social democracies across the Atlantic, where, in return for higher taxes and without any diminution of civil liberty, people buy themselves excellent public education, anxiety-free health care, and decent public transportation."[1] But rather than defending the idea that there might be something useful to be learned from European experiences with similar problems, the Democrats defensively denied any such intentions. In a kind of "Who, me?" reaction, they denied being Europhiles and certainly denied being guilty of being socialists.

Democrats knew the political lessons of American exceptionalism. Never admit to looking to other countries for ideas on how to reform your own. It is an attitude that has cost the United States dearly in social progress. It relies on keeping substantial parts of the public believing that they have the best possible living standard in the world, when they do not.

At the same time, those who work in policy studies routinely look to the experiences of other countries for ideas. They know that other countries have more successfully addressed a number of central social problems that continue to plague the United States. This book is an example.

When the Great Recession hit (see the new afterword for this edition), a few writers such as Paul Krugman in the *New York Times* looked at how Europeans were coping, compared to Americans, given their much more developed social safety nets. But most did not.

The contentious national debate over health care could not avoid some references to European and Canadian experiences at successfully insuring their whole populations at lower costs. But as the bills developed, American exceptionalism seemed to dominate discourse: Americans would solve—or not solve—it in their own way. The results of that effort are described and analyzed in chapter 13. Suffice it to say for now that even when health reform is fully implemented, the American system will still pale in comparison to European ones in terms of coverage, costs, and outcomes.

I have updated this edition with the latest available statistical information.

Preface

Americans would have been stunned by the headline in a Spanish newspaper: "Government Wants to Convert Assistance to Dependent Persons into the Fourth Pillar of the Welfare State."[1] At a time when entitlement programs had long been in the crosshairs of American public policy, with both the Democratic and Republican parties attacking them as wasteful, unaffordable, and ill conceived, the government of Spain, a country in the second rank of European prosperity, was precisely intending to build an entirely new major one. More revealing still was that the newspaper used the concept "welfare state" as a noncontroversial fact of life, unlike in the United States where it connotes a negative state of affairs to be avoided at all costs.

Americans have been trained to shudder at the very idea of a welfare state. As individualists, they find the thought of accepting public assistance repugnant, a sign of failure. Europeans, on the contrary, view a welfare state as being a benefit to all members of society. Middle- as well as lower-class persons benefit from free health care, and everyone benefits if the welfare state insures social cohesion and peace in the population. The U.S. abhorrence of developing an extensive welfare state is directly related to its having the highest murder and crime rates in the western world. Instead of investing in a welfare state, it invests in a prison system, with the result being that it now has the highest incarceration rate in the world.

European social programs provide safety nets so that downturns in economic life, such as unemployment, or in physical life, such as accidents and sickness, are not economically ruinous. But if Europe finds virtue in government programs providing basic social security, the United States finds it in the opposite: insecurity. It has a system of minimal social safety guards, seeming to believe that the fear of economic ruination propels economic productivity from its citizens.

One of the consequences of the American culture of economic and social insecurity is a national obsession with getting rich quick through winning lotteries or the hope that opportunity will come knocking in the form of getting rich through a successful lawsuit. The heightened litigiousness of the United States results in its having the highest per capita number of lawyers in the developed world.[2] Becoming rich, aside from dramatically improving material living standards, is the surest way to escape the country's omnipresent economic and social insecurity.

At the same time Americans, and those attracted to the American model in Europe, point to the double facts that the U.S. economy has been growing at a faster rate than the European economy and that it has a lower rate of unemployment. They interpret these facts as proof that the extensive European welfare state has weakened economic performance. They argue further that the high taxes necessary to support the welfare state divert capital from private investment and provide a disincentive for Europeans to work hard.

These arguments, though, are built upon a fundamental fallacy: that growth of the gross domestic product (GDP) is a perfect measure of a society's economic and social performance. GDP is a measure of the total goods and services produced within a society. It does not, however, distinguish between useful and harmful goods, or between necessary and unnecessary ones. If I suffer a robbery and then go out and spend a lot of money on security devices for my house, GDP grows. But we would hardly say that something good has happened. If I spend a lot of money at fast-food restaurants on supersized meals and then have to spend even more money to pay for the negative consequences to my health, GDP grows. But we would hardly say that it has grown for good reasons.

Just as a body can grow a cancer that threatens its overall health and survival, consumerist societies can grow in ways that are not socially healthy. Faster rates of GDP growth may produce more employment, but the question is employment doing what? If it is employment that is fulfilling to workers and socially useful to society, it is one thing. If it is employment at unfulfilling jobs that produce harmful or wasteful goods or services, it is quite another.

Economic growth, thus, in and of itself is not a panacea. It is the *type* of growth that counts. Societies can take either a laissez-faire approach to economic growth or one that attempts to guide it as much as possible in the public interest.

This is a book about different approaches—primarily American and European—to solving major social problems through the development of relevant social policies. While a major theme is to point out the much greater development and, I believe, advantages of European approaches over the approach of the United States, I do not wish to imply that these are stark night-and-day differences.

There are clear overlaps between the approaches, with some American programs—most notably the Social Security system—being appropriate bases for developing a more comprehensive and adequate set of social programs in the United States. The issue is not to develop a European approach in the United States. Rather, it is primarily to build on some of the programs and principles already in place so as to bring the United States up to western world standards of health care, family support, poverty reduction, and other social programs designed to deal with common outstanding social problems. If Europeans can develop social programs that are successful in diminishing social problems, so too can Americans.

Not so long ago, those of us brought up during the Cold War years saw the future in terms of capitalism versus socialism. Surely, 1989, a historical year, changed all of that. The disintegration of most of the "actually existing" socialist countries has removed socialism as a viable option for completely reorganizing societies for at least the near future. That does not mean, however, that socialism is dead. Who knows whether at some point in the years ahead it may reemerge as an alternative socioeconomic system? For the present, though, the competition has shifted from capitalism versus socialism to competition between alternative models of capitalism—between capitalist societies with comprehensive welfare states, as represented by those in Western Europe, and those with weak ones, as represented by the United States. It is a competition between models that allow socialist, or at least semi-socialist, solutions to capitalist problems and those that doggedly insist on maintaining or attaining as pure a capitalism as possible. If socialism is off the present world stage as a complete model, it still has a role to play in terms of developing ways to humanize capitalism as much as possible and perhaps preparing the way for some future development of a humane, prosperous, and democratic socialism.

I was fortunate to have the help of a number of people during the research on this project. María Asunción Merino Hernando and Elda Evangelina González of the History Institute at the Consejo Superior de Investigaciones Científicas in Madrid arranged for and generously helped me at every step during a two-month stay to work on this book. Csaba Szalo and Radim Marada of Masaryk University in the Czech Republic, at their annual conference on Conflict in Identities/Identities in Conflict, gave me an opportunity to expound and discuss the ideas in this book before Eastern Europeans. The Salzburg Seminar in Salzburg, Austria, subsidized a large part of my expenses to attend an important gathering on European migration issues. The text greatly benefited from the careful reading and suggestions of Levon Chorbajian. Through all of this I was helped in direct and indirect ways by friends who lent critical ears: Tim Black, Corey Dolgon, Mary Erdmans, Carolyn Howe, Jerry Lembcke, and Robert R. J. Ross. I have also derived valuable advice from my colleagues at Eastern Connecticut State University who have been participants in our ongoing research brown-bag meetings: Dennis Canterbury, Erica Chito Childs, Kimberly Dugan, Mary Kenny, Margaret Martin, Eunice Mathews, Andrew Nilsson, Ricardo Pérez, and Theresa Severance.

1

Introduction: From Social Problems to Social Policies

Human beings are problem-solving animals. Our days and biographies are filled with struggling to solve the problems of our existences. If it snows, we must shovel to get out the door. If sickness strikes, we must find a way to get well. We seek continually to resolve our small and large, routine and not so routine problems. But we never reach a plateau of a problem-free existence. For sure, we can resolve certain problems and lessen others, but we will never be without problems until we are dead. To live, then, is to struggle to resolve the problems of our existences.

When individuals face certain types of common problems that arise out of their interrelationships, we speak of social problems. Individuals may then join together in community groups or societies as wholes to address and solve such social problems as poverty, ethnic conflict, family breakdown, and drug abuse. The histories of societies, like the biographies of individuals, are filled with struggles to resolve the basic problems of their existence. And as with individuals, societies may resolve certain problems and lessen others, but they will never completely eliminate their problems. As each society evolves or changes, so too does the nature of its social problems. What remains constant is that there will always be social problems, for human beings are a problem-solving species.

Do humans, though, have the mental capacity to rationally identify and think out solutions to their common social problems? Are humans imbued with enough reason for the task? Or are human beings fundamentally irrational, doomed to only make matters worse by attempting to resolve their social problems? There has been a long and contentious

1

debate—the subject of chapter 2—over these issues in history and social thought.

Assuming for the moment that humans do have sufficient abilities to develop reasonable understandings of their common social problems, the question becomes one of how they go about identifying the central problems of their societies and proposing ways to resolve them. What people see as problematic within a society to a large extent depends upon how their minds have been trained to see. A racist sees no problem with racial prejudice and discrimination. Advocates of racial equality see it differently. How one perceives, then, is often as important as what one sees when it comes to the analysis and understanding of social problems.

STRUCTURAL CONTEXTS

All social problems occur within given structural contexts of historical background, technological stage of development, and socioeconomic system. These contexts may cause the very existence of particular types of social problems. In all cases they determine many of the problem's characteristics.

By *historical background*, it is meant that knowledge of how particular social problems have developed over time is essential. The problems of inner cities in the United States, for example, have developed historically according to particular logics in which immigration, both of foreigners and domestic rural populations, and emigration of middle classes to suburbs have played definite roles.

Technological stage of development refers to the movement in recent centuries from agriculturally based to industrially based societies, and then to what some call the postindustrial societies of Europe and the United States.[1] Industrialization, beginning in the late 1700s, remolded the social institutions of Europe and then spread to other parts of the world. With it came the elimination of certain types of social problems and the creation of new ones, including those associated with the development of large cities, itself caused by the location of industrial factories there. As third-world societies today are being transformed from agricultural to industrial technological bases, they are experiencing a number of the social problems that Europe and the United States went through when they were initially industrializing, including crowded cities and chaotic housing conditions. Among the responses to these social problems is migration, legally or illegally, to Europe or the United States, which then generates new social problems as well as opportunities for the migrants and receiving societies.

Socioeconomic system refers to the type of economic and social class system that is in place. In the twentieth century, that meant capitalist or socialist. The ending of Eastern and Central European socialist societies by the early 1990s, and the implementation of market reforms in China and other remaining socialist societies, resulted in a largely capitalist world economy. But there are still differences between types of capitalist societies.

Western Europe and the United States today represent different models for structuring high-income capitalist societies. The balances between state (or public) and privately based economic sectors are different, with the state having a much greater role in economic activities in Europe than in the United States. European societies have large welfare states that socialize key consumption expenses such as health, retirement, and child care for their populations, while the United States attempts to minimize such public expenditures.

SOCIAL THEORY AND IDEOLOGY

If how we see is, consciously or not, built upon theoretical assumptions that we hold about the nature of social reality and how to understand that reality, then issues within social theory necessarily enter into the study of social problems. Philosophic, psychological, and in some cases originally religion-based theoretical assumptions of what human beings are capable of—the subjects of chapters 2 and 3—define or limit the extent to which it is believed possible to fully resolve central social problems. If a person believes that human beings are innately aggressive, as Sigmund Freud did, then he or she is likely to also believe that violence, up to and including war, can at best be reined in but never abolished. If a person believes, following Jean-Jacques Rousseau's dictum in *The Social Contract*, that "man is born free and everywhere he is in chains," then it becomes possible and desirable to remove the chains.

Social theory is particularly important in how social problems are perceived—the subject of chapter 4. Certain theoretical concepts and ideas allow us to penetrate often-misleading surface appearances of social problems to uncover and reveal their underlying realities. It may be a commonsense belief that the poor are responsible for their condition. A theoretical examination of the nature of the society will indicate otherwise: poverty is better understood as a more structurally than individually caused condition.

As I hope to make clear, many of the core debates about how to approach social problems in Europe and the United States have been generated by critical concepts in the theories of Karl Marx and Emile Durkheim.

From Marx comes an understanding of the relationship between commodification and social problems in capitalist societies, with the implied notion of decommodification as an antidote. From Durkheim comes the emphasis on social solidarity, which is the origin of the contemporary social policy concept of social inclusion.

The relationship between the concerns of social theory and those of the western political ideologies of conservatism, liberalism, and socialism is close. Social theory in its most academic guise pretends to be scientific and nonpolitical. The reality is that both it and ideology draw their ideas from the common source of western social thought, and both focus on the nature of the problems confronting societies.

Ideology is an applied form of social thinking. It orients what political actors struggle to attain. It is the nexus between generalized ideas about how to treat social problems and the development of relevant state programs.

SOCIAL POLICY

Once societies have identified their outstanding social problems, they usually develop relevant public social policies—the subject of chapter 6. They may also do nothing, choosing a laissez-faire approach or one of benign neglect. But where public action is taken, there are policy alternatives. Politics—who has power and whose choices prevail—and ideology inevitably enter into which alternatives are chosen. The goals of social policy are inherently ideological. From one ideological point of view, social inequality is an abomination to be eradicated; from another, it is the carrot-and-stick mechanism that ensures economic progress. Conservative, liberal, and socialistically inclined goals motivate the different policy options.

COMPARING EUROPE AND THE UNITED STATES

When we speak of the approach to a particular social problem in the United States, it is clear enough what we are referring to, since the United States is a particular country. But it is not at all that clear when we speak of a European approach. The European part of the Eurasian continent begins at the Ural Mountains in Russia and the Emba River in Kazakhstan. It includes forty-four countries or parts of countries, each with its own set of social policies.

All of these countries, though, are not in our unit of analysis. Rather, it is what was referred to during the Cold War as the Western European countries, which were organized capitalistically and had, along with the United States and Japan, the world's highest average standards of living. They were distinguishable from the communist Eastern European countries, which had lower average standards of living as well as different economic and political systems.

What is important for us is that the origin of a model of capitalism with a comprehensive welfare state began in the Western European countries and continues to be most highly developed there. It is the model that today represents a sharp alternative to the so-called Washington neoliberal or neoconservative—terms that mean the same in conventional usage despite their seeming difference—consensus.

The East-West ideological division died with the end of the Cold War in 1989. The United Nations classifies the formerly communist countries as transitional societies—transitioning from socialism to capitalism. They now represent a lower-income variety of European capitalist societies. With the exception of Slovenia, none of the formerly European communist countries are high-income according to World Bank standards, though a number of them have welfare states as legacies of their communist pasts that are closer to the Western European than to the American model.

As for the former Western Europe category, it has been supplanted by the development in the early 1990s of the European Union (EU). The EU originally comprised fifteen countries. Then in 2004 it expanded to twenty-five, including some of the formerly communist countries.[2] Not all of the original Western European countries are members of the EU, though. Switzerland and Norway are notable nonmembers. Through all of these shifting category boundaries, we will keep our focus for comparative purposes with the United States on the EU-15, plus Norway and Switzerland, as the model of advanced capitalist development with a strong welfare state.

There is an intense struggle occurring over the future of the welfare state in the post-1989 world order. When American secretary of defense Donald Rumsfeld distinguished "old" from "new" Europe in the buildup to the Iraq War, he was attempting to denigrate Western European countries that opposed Washington's policy and praising formerly communist Eastern European countries that supported it. A hidden meaning was that the Eastern European countries should follow Washington's leadership on social policy as well and trim back their welfare states.

Two models of developed capitalism thus confront each other in the post-1989 world order. High taxes and generous social benefits characterize one, and low taxes and minimal social benefits characterize the other. Beyond these defining differences, there are numerous others in terms of assumptions and conceptions of social progress. Some of these differences will be apparent in terms of theoretical and political orientations discussed in chapters 2 through 5. Others will become apparent in discussions of overall social policy in chapters 6 and 7, as well as in comparative treatments of the particular social problems of inequality, poverty, unemployment, family issues, health care, racial and ethnic conflict, and crime, covered in chapters 8 through 15. In chapter 16, I will summarize with a list of principles for orienting the approaches to progressive social policy on both sides of the Atlantic.

2

The Social Worldview of Medieval Christianity as Prologue

Medieval Christian religiosity was impressive with the sway it held over whole populations, undoubtedly more powerful than the hold today of religions in either Europe or the United States. This is evidenced by any trip to an art museum where European paintings earlier than the 1500s are almost exclusively consumed with religious themes. Medieval artists directed all of their talents toward portraying what was believed on the basis of faith.

The religiosity of the Middle Ages fits into what Emile Durkheim, the late nineteenth- and early twentieth-century French sociologist, called a collective conscience—a belief system of ideas held in common by average members of a society.[1] In his analysis, medieval European societies, as well as other societies in other regions of the world that existed in similar conditions, required a strong belief system to provide the basis of social order. That belief system united men and women over large areas when markets, roads, and other forms of uniting them were lacking.

In the religion-dominated thinking of the Middle Ages, the ethereal soul was the central identifying characteristic of human beings, with faith being the basis of knowledge. Though humans could not directly apprehend the meanings of either one, they provided links, however mysterious, to God, the source of all ultimate meaning. Men and women marveled at, rather than sought to understand, the mysteries that enshrouded them. Behind them all was a benevolent God. Theology and philosophy were fused. Human reason played a distinctly secondary role to faith, used only to deepen understanding of what was understood on the basis of the latter.[2]

From the time of Christ until the fourth century, Christianity had been an outlaw religion within the Roman Empire, its believers often persecuted. Those conditions affected its core beliefs, which challenged earthly social and political hierarchies. Shared dangerous living conditions, as well as deep common religious beliefs, bonded together the outlaw Christian communities. They willingly endured these ways of life because of deep beliefs in the righteousness of their movement, and to some extent they saw themselves as social equals. But when Rome's rulers embraced Christianity in the fourth century and made it a state religion, the shared conditions of illegality and persecution vanished. Under new conditions of political acceptance, Christians were less likely to live ways of life that challenged conventional social hierarchies.

Augustine of Hippo, later Saint Augustine, writing from the late fourth to the early fifth century, is a key figure in the transition of Christianity from outlaw to state religion. His writings contain much that could be used to justify acceptance of social hierarchies, though that was not his primary intent.

Augustine developed the concept of predestination, which had been briefly mentioned but not elaborated into importance by the Apostle Paul, to challenge the Pelagian notion that humans had free will to choose good over evil and thereby obtain salvation. To choose good, according to Augustine, requires the aid or grace of God. God, though, did not spread grace equally among humans. This was indicated by the existence of both good and evil, with different humans practicing more the one than the other. Since God has foreknowledge of all, it follows that God has predestined which humans will receive grace.[3] No longer, then, are humans strictly equal before God, as most early Christians had believed.

Augustine emphasized that human evil began with the Fall and original sin, as told in the book of Genesis in the Bible. God created Adam and then Eve and placed them in the Garden of Eden, an earthly paradise. Since all was bountiful and blissful in Eden, there was neither good nor evil. For good to exist, there must be evil against which it is contrasted and vice versa. God commanded Adam and Eve not to eat from the apple tree. Eve succumbed to temptation and ate the forbidden fruit and then enticed Adam to do the same. They went against the commandment of God—the meaning of sin. Human beings ever since have inherited this original guilt and sin. Social problems as such arise, not from given social arrangements, but because of the problematic human condition itself.[4]

Much more important than the doctrine of predestination for medieval social assumptions were Augustine's teachings on celestial and temporal order. God created the world and existence of humans and all other organic and inorganic matter with purpose. Everything in the temporal world reflects God's design even if it does not seem to. The existence of evil, for example, would appear to be against God's will, and that is one of the meanings of evil. At the same time, though, evil serves to test humans' resolve to resist and overcome it.

There is thus a Creator who stands above everything else, a hierarchy to the celestial order. From that, Augustine deduced that there should be a hierarchy to the temporal order as well: "The peace of all things is the tranquility of order. Order is the distribution which allots things equal and unequal, each to its own place."

Augustine embraced what later would be called in the modern social sciences the organic analogy, in which the logic of the social world is believed to be the same as that of organic bodies, where each part plays a role in the survival of the whole body. These are both parallel logics of organic relations and organic logics within encompassing organic logics. The soul is superior to the body, as temporal rulers are to the ruled. The logic of existence is organic harmony of unequal parts: "The peace of the body then consists in the duly proportioned arrangement of its parts."[5]

In his most stark formulation, Augustine wrote,

> They who care for the rest rule—the husband the wife, the parents the children, the masters the servants; and they who are cared for obey—the women their husbands, the children their parents, the servants their masters.

To modern eyes, Augustine's organic harmony offends. He justified male domination and slavery as God-ordained, and he completely eschewed any principle of democratic participation and selection of leaders. Nevertheless, he interpreted it as authority that should be based on organic reciprocity, not narrow power differences. Rulers owe to the ruled mercy and care, while the ruled owe obedience. Rulers are not to be tyrants since they are to rule for, as well as over, the ruled. When they do so, they produce temporal harmony that mirrors celestial harmony.

> Those who rule serve those whom they seem to command; for they rule not from a love of power, but from a sense of the duty they owe to others—not because they are proud of authority, but because they love mercy.[6]

Rulers must rule also because original sin causes there to be evil in the world. The ruler has the responsibility to maintain good. Good in turn means keeping humans constantly focused on God and God's purpose for them. Since original sin makes humans fallible, it is the purpose of rulers to hold that fallibility in check. In part, this was written at a time when Augustine saw rulers as combining both political and religious functions. And indeed, throughout the medieval period, political rulers would see themselves in unity with the church as defenders of the faith, tensions between themselves and religious figures notwithstanding.

What is most important about Augustine is his emphasis on an organic hierarchical community in which, by implication, inequality is proper. But it is an inequality in which the powerful have obligations to the less powerful—the basis of noblesse oblige. At the same time, the less powerful are not to rebel against this arrangement. They are to keep their eyes, minds, and faith on the greater celestial purpose of leading spiritually focused lives.

This is at once the future feudal principle of both the personal bonds of vassalage among the nobility that Marc Bloch so much stressed[7] and the attitude of noblesse oblige professed by the nobility toward their peasants. Because social hierarchies in terms of authority—but not necessarily in terms of wealth—are manifestations of God's hierarchical order, they are not to be challenged or resisted. Augustine acknowledged that social injustices could exist in the temporal world because of the consequences of original sin, but he counseled Christians not to challenge these injustices. Christians were to maintain their faith while accepting their social fates.

The effect of Augustine's teachings was to prepare the way for the medieval orthodoxy that God intended for there to be social inequality in earthly existence. The prevailing medieval assumption would be that people were born unequally as natural superiors and inferiors. It followed that if humans were naturally unequal, then inequality should rule also in the political and social spheres. The medieval aristocracy would justify its rule and privileges with the claim that they were naturally superior and therefore ought to exercise power. There was no conception of democracy inasmuch as it would run counter to what was assumed to be a social order based on the natural order. The word *aristocracy* itself (from the Greek *aristos*, or "the best," and *kratos*, or "rule") meant rule of the best.

The medieval conception of natural inequality rationalized the realities of actual economic, social, and political inequality in a double way. To the aristocracy it gave a useful church-backed justification. Their domination was not an imposition on society but rather was in harmony with the natural order of things. To the peasantry it gave solace that God had ordained their lot.

Sixteenth-century precursors of later racist ideologists, building upon the medieval conception of natural inequality, extended the notion of natural superiors and inferiors to race. In this application, *superior* and *inferior* referred to whole races of people. Just as the medieval conception was a rationalization in the sphere of ideas for the realities of economic and political inequality, the race-based application rationalized the realities of the European conquest of the Americas and the expansion of black slavery.

The assumption of God-willed natural inequality up through the 1600s was thus the basis for justifying the inequality of lower classes and of the increasingly oppressed races. Inequality existed legally by people having unequal status before the law, politically by lacking a recognized democratic right to equal voting, and socially by people living at different levels.

Later, the Augustinian and medieval culture of an organic community order based on hierarchy and obedience, but with obligations of the higher to the lower classes, would culturally mutate into contemporary European conservative acceptance of the welfare state. Conservatives would be able to see in the welfare state a way to socialize their obligations to the less privileged. The medieval, originally Catholic, notion of social obligation, though, did not make the passage unaltered across the Atlantic, where took root a culture—greatly molded by Protestants—of unfettered individualism, which would interfere with the development of social obligation and state social spending.

3

Secular Transitions
and Assumptions

After the religion-centered medieval period, new currents of secular-based social thinking gradually emerged that coexisted with traditional theological thinking. Niccolò Machiavelli's *The Prince*, published in the early sixteenth century, was the first prominent theory of governance that contained no theological references or justifications. The terms of the issues were gradually shifting from sacred to secular, albeit substantial portions of the population continued to embrace religious worldviews that affected how they perceived social issues.

The modern secular urge to reform societies to eliminate social problems has fired the hopes of reformers and revolutionaries alike. Emile Durkheim, the French sociologist, believed that governments could greatly reduce the incidence of social problems through careful social planning. Karl Marx, the nineteenth-century revolutionary, believed that once socialism was achieved, the outstanding problems of human want and class strife that had plagued the species for thousands of years would be vanquished. Others, though, have been less optimistic in their assumptions of what is possible, in large part because of fundamentally different conceptions of what human beings are capable of achieving socially.

At the heart of these differences are polar opposite classical assumptions about the social nature of human beings, differences that had precursors in medieval Christianity: Are human beings fundamentally equal or unequal? At one level this is a question about whether humans are born equal or unequal. At another level, regardless of assumptions about innate qualities, it concerns legal and political equality, equality of opportunity, and equality of living conditions.

Are humans born good or with negative (the secular equivalent of evil) characteristics? Those who assume that humans are innately good accept the Rousseauian formulation that social problems result from the way societies are organized, not the way humans are. If humans are born good, then it is a question of reforming their institutions to bring them into alignment with that goodness. Those who assume that humans are born evil believe that reforms can have, at best, only limited success in preventing or resolving social problems and making societies better. What is innate cannot be reformed socially.

Are humans rational or irrational? Those who hold that humans essentially function on the basis of reason accept the Enlightenment belief that humans have the mental abilities to reason out solutions to the problems of their social existences. Those who hold that humans are essentially irrational believe that rationally planned social reforms, as well intentioned as they may be, are doomed either to make things worse by constraining irrational but natural needs or, at best, to have limited success.

EQUALITY

Thomas Hobbes, who had an otherwise unfavorable view of human nature as evil and aggressive, concluded that such differences as there were among humans were not enough to establish that they were innately unequal:

> Nature hath made men so equall, in the faculties of body, and mind; as that though there bee found one man sometimes manifestly stronger in body, or of quicker mind than another; yet when all is reckoned together, the difference between man, and man, is not so considerable, as that one man can thereupon claim to himselfe any benefit, to which another may not pretend, as well as he.

Those who are physically weak are not so physically weak that they cannot kill the stronger. There was in Hobbes's reckoning even more equality in mental faculties, for "every man is contented with his share," thinking that he is as wise as any other.[1] John Locke, who held a more favorable view of the natural state of humans, agreed that they were equal.[2] Inequality, as such, in the thinking of Hobbes and Locke arose for social, not natural, reasons.

Later egalitarian thinkers would conceive of natural equality more in terms of potential worth to society than of physical or mental makeup. To conclude that humans are born with an equal potential worth to society is not the same as concluding that there are no physical or mental differences among them. Even at that, the physical and mental differences that there are among humans are not as great as the differences within other species such as dogs. According to this egalitarian position, such physical and mental differences as there are cannot be construed in a single hierarchy, with one being worth more than another to society. People have different strengths and weaknesses. A woman who cannot run fast may be able to add numbers quickly.

Acceptance of the natural condition of human beings as that of equality on whatever basis, however, does not automatically lead to believing that there should be social equality. It may or may not. While early nineteenth-century socialists argued that humans are born equal and should be socially equal in life, others accepted that humans are born equal but argued that only a minority worked hard and thus should be rewarded more than the rest for doing so.

The counter position is to assume that there is significant natural inequality among humans that social orders must take into account. This polar position is that of Friederich Nietzsche. In his view, the mass of people never rise above being driven by base instincts. Only a few exceptional individuals have the qualities—most especially a "will to power"—to form the elites that guide societies and activities within them, such as the arts. These elites have much greater worth to society than do the "lower men."

Theories of equality, according to Nietzsche, contradict unequal human nature; they manifest the resentment that the weak hold toward their natural superiors. The early Christian belief that the meek shall inherit the earth represents, in Nietzsche's most audacious interpretation, the irrational resentment of Roman slaves, not a cry for justice by oppressed people. It is the resentful whine of the natural inferiors of society, those who properly were slaves rather than masters.

Nietzsche variously referred to ordinary people as the mob, the herd, the mass, lower men, or the herd mass, contrasting them with higher men, the aristocratic, the ruling race, and the exceptional. He advocated the creation of future overmen who would combine the sublime virtues of philosophers and artists and would exercise iron self-discipline. Between "exceptional men" and the mob exist mediocre people who often rule. Universal suffrage, in which all are allowed equal votes, works in favor of the herd and bleeds the greatness out of societies. In a telling comment, Nietzsche stated that the main objective is "not to see the task of the higher species in leading the lower (as, for example, Comte does), but the lower as a base upon which the higher species performs it own tasks—upon which it stands."[3]

Though he believed that at least some of the positive traits of higher men were inheritable, he was ambiguous on the question of whether the higher men emerged as a result of genetic stock, genetic chance, or through their own will to power or making. Whatever the case, it was clear in his mind that ordinary people should defer to the higher men. There was no equality between human beings, except perhaps within the categories of the herd and higher men.

Other theorists of natural inequality have been less stark. By the end of the nineteenth century, a new ideology of inequality based on alleged differences in intelligence capacities began to take hold in Europe and the United States. According to this view, native intelligence is the most important attribute of humans, and they are born with unequal capacities for it.

Emile Durkheim is representative of this line of thought. He believed that hierarchical divisions of labor and social inequality in societies needed to correspond to the unequal distribution of intellectual talents in populations. The best functioning social system would be one in which "social inequalities exactly express natural inequalities."[4]

For Durkheim, a primary task of science was to measure the intelligence levels of children in order to determine how they would be educated. Those with higher capabilities would be given advanced educational training, and those with lower capabilities more basic training. Presumably the hierarchy of differential educational training would match the hierarchy of differential societal needs.

At the time he was developing his conception of human inequality based on intelligence—the early 1890s—there were only crude and grossly inaccurate attempts to determine intelligence differences by measuring sizes of skulls. By the end of the nineteenth century, such dubious external measures had been supplanted by the development of intelligence testing, which led to IQ tests.

By the end of the twentieth century, assumed intelligence differences would become the most widely held basis for assumptions of natural inequality. Theorists of intelligence, though, are not in agreement over whether existing tests validly measure intelligence or about whether intelligence is susceptible to conceptualization on a single hierarchical scale.

Most contemporary opponents of social equality continue to base their beliefs on the assumption that humans are naturally unequal and therefore have unequal capacities to contribute to societies. That humans have different physical and mental capacities is clear enough. But for most human beings those differences fall within a relatively narrow range. It is more useful to see humans as having uneven rather than unequal capacities. A gifted surgeon can be an inept parent, an artist terrible at mathematics, an insightful social researcher musically tone deaf and unable to carry a tune, or a business executive incapable of understanding and carrying out a simple repair to her or his household plumbing. The all-around excellent person does not exist. Even Benjamin Franklin had his faults and ineptitudes. If societies need many types of skills, then it is arbitrary to reward some over others.

GOOD AND EVIL

Secularization transformed good and evil from obedience or disobedience of God's will to actions toward fellow human beings, to whether humans were more inclined to be helpful and caring or to be egoistic and hostile toward others.

Thomas Hobbes and Jean-Jacques Rousseau approached the question in much the same manner. Each reasoned that it was necessary to distinguish the natural from the social qualities of humans in order to determine whether they were essentially good or evil. They assumed that the first humans lived isolated from each other and were therefore unsocialized in nature. Only later did they come together and develop social institutions. It followed that human nature could be seen in its clearest relief among the earliest unsocialized humans.

Despite following a similar reasoning process, Hobbes and Rousseau drew different conclusions. Hobbes found early humans to be living solitary, "nasty, short and brutish" lives in which they were egocentric and aggressive toward others, living in a condition of "war of every man against every man."[5] Each man was the other's wolf. Like the religious view, Hobbes held that the state was necessary to hold this natural tendency in check. Rousseau also believed that the earliest humans led solitary lives, but contrary to Hobbes he believed them to have sentiments of altruism and love. According to him, such evil characteristics as found by Hobbes only developed as a result of later social institutions.[6]

Karl Marx would later critique the assumptions of both. The original natural condition was not one of solitary existence of individuals who only later came together on the basis of social compacts to form societies. Rather, the earliest humans existed from the beginning within groups. Group identity took overwhelming precedence over individual identity.[7] The notion of the individual apart from the group is a modern notion. While Marx agreed with Rousseau that negative human features resulted from negative social institutions, he was not inclined to go along with his implied anthropological view.

John Locke took the view that humans were by nature neither good nor evil. Rather, they came into this world as tabulae rasae or blank sheets, which could be molded in either direction.[8] Beyond its overly passive notion of human nature as entirely plastic, the Lockean notion carried over and was consistent with Marx's later emphasis that humans make their histories and have the capacity to create social institutions that encourage either positive or negative behaviors.

While the issue of good and evil developed a secular form in the hands of Hobbes, Locke, Rousseau, Machiavelli, and others, the original sacred form in which it was posed remained a strong if no longer monopolistic and dominant tendency within popular social assumptions. That was why Marx considered religious thinking to be a great obstacle to what he called scientific socialism. And today in the United States, the Christian conservative movement bases its interventions in politics on its literal reading of Christian doctrine, as does the Vatican worldwide. Both continue to influence popular social thinking, which in turn influences how politicians approach social policy issues.

Altruism and individualism are the secular reflexes of religious good and evil. Those who hold that altruistic concern for others as either an innate or achievable human quality believe that humans function better when they live within economic and social structures that encourage cooperation and sharing with others. Those who hold that the motive of individualistic self-gain is an innate human quality believe that the best social and economic orders are those that maximize individual freedom to gain without regard for others.

Adam Smith in *The Wealth of Nations* advanced the famous proposition that individuals seeking to maximize their own interests fuel the growth of capitalist economies. Rather than producing a chaotic struggle of all against all, the effect of competitive individualism is to create what he called an invisible hand that produces order and mutual benefit. (Karl Marx would later castigate the invisible hand as an alienated commodity or market fetishism that was oppressive.) Smith's assumption was that humans are innately egoistic. That proposition continues to be an ultimate fallback argument for opponents of social equality and comprehensive welfare states. Without inequality of market rewards, humans would not be motivated to produce, and without humans being motivated and driven to produce, economies fail.[9]

There is no evidence, though, that humans have always needed monetary gain to motivate themselves to work. Even the most ardent individualist will have to admit that many work hard more for their families than for themselves. Otherwise, why would parvenus care about continuing to build up fortunes to pass on to heirs long after they have accumulated enough to live on comfortably for the rest of their own lives? More importantly, many get pleasure out of helping communities through volunteer work without thought of monetary gain.

History has witnessed quite different motivations for human conduct. Max Weber classically argued that Calvinists worked hard, not for monetary gain, but because they thought that by doing so, they were fulfilling their God-ordained calling or purpose in life.[10] Weber also emphasized that in addition to monetary gain, power and status gains have also motivated human conduct.[11] There are multiple examples of people who enjoy exercising power even if it does not bring particular monetary rewards. While that motivation can lead to authoritarianism and present a problem for democracy, it indicates that humans can work hard for other than monetary rewards. Guillermo Bonfil Batalla argues persuasively that indigenous communities in Mexico confound western modernizers because status accumulates within them by generously giving away money through sponsorship of elaborate religious and other community celebrations rather than by becoming personally rich. The Indians strive for status rather than money.[12]

Motivations are more culturally formed and variable than set in any innate human disposition. To argue that the egalitarian principle of the welfare state contradicts human nature is to reify the variable and creative possibilities of human nature itself. It is to reify one noticeable cultural effect of social Darwinian capitalism. To the contrary, a strong egalitarian welfare state can help to mold new egalitarian and socially inclusive cultures. In the end, it is an argument about the type of culture that humans wish to live within and encourage.

REASON AND IRRATIONALITY

Throughout the Renaissance, conceptions of the purposes and capabilities of human knowledge gradually shifted away from being exclusively religiously centered. The transition culminated with the eighteenth-century Enlightenment. Reason completed its overthrow of faith, divine right, and tradition as guiding principles. For leading thinkers, true knowledge of how to order their lives and societies now had to meet the test of reason based on what was provable by logic or experience.

The Enlightenment gave birth to the idea that humans could use reason to progressively perfect their societies. They did not have to passively accept whatever existed socially under the belief that it had been God ordained. Nor did they have to accept a given social arrangement because of a supposed divine right of kings. All that existed secularly was susceptible to judgment by human reason. While some Enlightenment thinkers retained a belief in God and others did not, all agreed that humans had the capacity to perfect the secular realm.

French Enlightenment thought received its greatest expression in the writings of Jean-Jacques Rousseau. In *The Social Contract*, Rousseau issued his famous observation that "man is born free, and everywhere he is in chains."[13] The natural condition of humans, according to Rousseau, is one of freedom and goodness, but societies corrupt that essence and make them unfree and bad. Rousseau's solution was not to return to some pre-social primitive nature, as is mistakenly assumed by many. Rather it was to use the human capacity to reason to change societies so that they would express rather than corrupt the inherent goodness of humans.

Enlightenment thinking influenced the intellectual climate that led to the French and American revolutions, both of which were fought to end the control of kings and usher in republican forms of government, that is, governments based upon secular, reason-based constitutions and laws rather than upon religious beliefs or individuals.

In Germany, Immanuel Kant devised a philosophical system that divided the knowable from the unknowable. The human mind, according to Kant, organized its experience of reality through categories of its making. We think in terms of words that are categories. If I see a four-legged creature that barks, I think "dog," since that is a category humans have invented that includes all four-legged creatures that bark. The human mind, however, is unable to go beyond the categories of perception and to directly comprehend reality. I cannot comprehend the full meaning of that particular dog—its history, feelings, thoughts if any, or reason for being. Underlying incomprehensible realities include the ultimate meaning of existence—why we are here—and God. The mind therefore resorts to reason to perfect its categories of perception while leaving to faith beliefs in what constitutes ultimate realities. By implication, men and women can strive for certainty over what reason can judge, but not over what it cannot.

Many of the leaders of the American War of Independence, including Benjamin Franklin, Thomas Jefferson, and Thomas Paine, were deists. They believed in God as the ultimate cause of human existence but believed that humans themselves were responsible for how they organized their social and political affairs. Like Kant, they separated dualistically what they were responsible for controlling with reason from what was beyond their control and comprehension. The American as well as French revolutions therefore led to the separation of church and state. Churches could be founded on religious beliefs and faith, but states had to be founded on reason.

While faith and religion-centered conceptions continued to exist among theologians and populations in general, they no longer held the monopoly position. Religion- and secular-based ways of seeing and interpreting the world now coexisted and contended with each other—both as movements struggling for hegemony and within the contradictory ways that men and women often composed their own worldviews.

That men and women could purposefully change their societies on the basis of reason was a path-breaking idea that set the agenda for nineteenth-century political, economic, and sociological theory. In political theory it led to attempts to replace autocratic with republican forms of governance. In place of the rule of powerful figures on the basis of their own whims, governments would be established on the basis of reasoned-out constitutions. Max Weber concluded that modern forms of governance rest on the belief of the governed that their political institutions follow reasonable rules rather than traditional practices or guidance, however gifted, of great charismatic leaders.[14] Economic theory from Adam Smith to John Stuart Mill incorporated utilitarian assumptions that human beings use reason to calculate how to proceed to their best advantages in market transactions.

Karl Marx was the most audacious inheritor of the Enlightenment imperative. In his theory, reason plays two roles. First, it exists in history. Societies rise and fall according to a definite logic that Marx believed he had discovered. Armed with knowledge of that logic, humans could now purposefully change their societies. They could not change them any way they pleased, but they could change them in accord with historical possibilities once those possibilities had been understood. Second, his conception of the human being embodied reason. What differentiates humans from other animals, in Marx's view, is that humans have the cerebral capacity to think creatively. Other animals construct and labor in other ways, but they do not do so consciously. Beavers build dams because they are born with the instinctual knowledge and drive to do so. Humans can only build dams if they learn how to do so, and that takes reasoned, creative thought and labor.

The main drift of Enlightenment and post-Enlightenment thought thus carried the assumption that humans are fundamentally rational and should use their capacity for reason to perfect their societies. But not everyone agreed.

Edmund Burke in *Reflections on the Revolution in France* questioned whether humans ought to use reason to remove traditional institutions that had met the tests of time. His anti-Enlightenment stance would inform early nineteenth-century conservatism. Vilfredo Pareto is representative of social thinking that assumes that humans are fundamentally irrational in their conduct but that the methods of science can be used to study and understand them as well as to develop reasonable social orders. Friedrich Nietzsche is representative of the complete irrationalist position. To him, irrational will and sentiments govern human conduct and are the bases for social order.

Auguste Comte, the founder of sociology in the 1840s, embraced the Enlightenment assumptions that humans are reasonable and that reason can be used to perfect societies. However, instead of seeing the perfection of societies in terms of applying future-oriented reforms, he saw it in terms of the Burkean conservative position of applying reforms to preserve traditional institutions that had met the tests of time.

Sigmund Freud's social theory represents a bridging of the irrationalist position. He assumed both rationalist and irrationalist elements in both the nature of human beings and in how they established their societies. For the twentieth century, his was the most important critique of Enlightenment assumptions that men and women could use reason to guide their social affairs and that they could progressively perfect their societies to eliminate misery. His main conclusion was that certain social problems were manifestations of innate, unchangeable, irrational psychological drives. Societies had to control these negative psychological characteristics—such as the need to be aggressive—in order for there to be a modicum of social order, a secular conclusion reminiscent of the medieval belief that governments exist to rein in human evil. The cost of social order, though, was frustrated psychological drives with resulting psychological misery. The march of civilization in constructing social order was also the march of psychological misery.

To understand Freud's social conclusion, we have to reconstruct his basic psychological theory. But before doing so it is worth recounting why he felt obliged to draw out the social consequences of his psychological theory. During the 1920s, Vienna, where Freud lived, had a popularly backed socialist government that embarked on ambitious social projects to resolve housing shortages and other problems afflicting workers. In this atmosphere, Wilhelm Reich, one of Freud's most gifted students, became a Marxist and then published an essay titled, "Dialectical Materialism and Psychoanalysis."[15] Reich argued that Marx was to social liberation what Freud was to psychological liberation, and that the two theories could be synthesized into one overall theory of human liberation. Freud disagreed profoundly and in reaction published his own view in *Civilization and Its Discontents.*[16] At roughly the same time, Albert Einstein, the physicist, was assigned by the League of Nations to conduct interviews with leading thinkers of the day to develop ideas for preventing war. Einstein wrote to Freud for his views. His reply was subsequently published as "Why War?" and in it he reiterated the central arguments of *Civilization and Its Discontents.*[17]

Freud argued in both that war exists because it manifests deep psychological, instinctual needs. Human beings are born, according to him, with two opposing bundles of instincts—the first he labeled Eros after the Greek god of love, the second Thanatos after the god of death. Eros represents life energy and has other- and inner-directed foci. Toward others, we have an instinctual need to have loving relations. Love, both platonic and sexual, is not just desire; it is also an instinctual need that has physiochemical, organic roots. But while we have an instinctual need to love, we cannot love whomever and at whatever time we wish. The other or others must agree. When they do not, a person must repress her or his desires. In a more general sense, people continually must repress this drive in order for particular social institutions to function. Erotic desires of participants in monogamous family relations may wander, but they learn to repress or not act upon these desires in order to preserve the relationship. If there was no repression whatsoever of sexual desires, then rape would be more widespread than it is. Psychological repression, in other words, is the price humans must pay for there to be social order.

In terms of our inner selves, each person has a drive toward self-preservation. We avoid death and other threats to our organism. Taken to the extreme, though, no person would leave her or his house in the morning for fear of meeting up with harm. In order to function we must put on hold or repress our instinct toward self-preservation.

Coming from the opposite direction is the death, or Thanatos, bundle of instincts. Aggression is its outward manifestation, self-destruction its inner manifestation. Toward others we get a certain satisfaction from being aggressive. A secret pleasure is felt upon hearing of the misfortune of others. The blaring of horns and contorting of faces at drivers who hesitate a second after a traffic signal changes feels good to many; otherwise they wouldn't do it. In American football, half an entire stadium can roar its approval at the sacking of the opposing quarterback, disregarding or perhaps approving of any physical injuries and suffering that may result. In its most lethal manifestation, the aggressive instinct fuels warfare and massacres.

But there could be no modicum of social order if individuals did not at least partially control their aggressive instincts. Repression keeps anger at others from turning into doing them direct physical harm. We all have our enemies, but we do not at all times physically lash out at them. Legal orders codify society's repression mechanism, spelling out the lines that must not be crossed.

Inwardly, the death instinct boomerangs with suicidal urges. There is a part of us that continually entertains the idea of death as desirable. In our most morose moments, we feel that life is not worth living. Each year a percentage of individuals act upon their self-destructive instincts and commit suicide. More prevalent is self-destructive behavior, as when individuals deliberately engage in high-risk activities or habits.

Eros and Thanatos are thus opposing contradictory instincts, according to Freud. There is a constant struggle between them, which results in the different balances that individuals have. The struggle is at play in the experience that many people have when they stand on a high rooftop or cliff looking over and have fleeting thoughts of jumping. But they don't—or at least most don't. A Freudian interpretation of this common experience would be to say that the death instinct comes out of the recesses of the mind and makes itself known when there is an opportunity to gratify itself. But it is held in check by the stronger self-preservation instinct.

We are not truly aware of all of the impact that these instincts have upon our psychological lives, according to Freud. The mind contains a part that he labeled the unconscious, and it is there that the instinctual activity originates. In introducing the idea of the unconscious, Freud broke with earlier psychology, which assumed that humans were fully aware of their thought processes, even if they were unreasonable ones. Freud, on the contrary, believed that much of our mental activity was based upon causes of which we are not aware. The role of the psychoanalyst was to help patients become aware of what was lodged in their minds. The psychoanalyst would listen to the patient on the couch describing anxieties or other causes of concern and then see patterns that revealed material lodged in the unconscious. Dreams and even slips of the tongue—"I could just kill myself" after a blunder— were material for the Freudian psychoanalyst that revealed unconscious drives. If we are not fully aware of what is in our minds that fuels our motivations, then we are, to that extent, not fully rational creatures.

Thus, at the center of the human existence for Freud was the contradiction between needs for psychological gratification and the imperatives of social order. Instinctual gratification taken to its logical conclusion undermines social order. Social order requires that instinctual needs be at least partially repressed. Repression in turn manifests itself in various degrees of psychological misery. There will therefore, in Freud's eyes, always be discontent with a given social order. Unlike Marx, who finds alienation resulting from the nature of the social order, Freud finds it arising from the inevitable contradiction between instinctual human needs and those of any social order. There is no way, through reform or revolutionary change, to eliminate the alienation.

Albert Einstein, seventeen years after receiving Freud's views on the inevitability of war, wrote an invited article for the inaugural issue of the American socialist magazine *Monthly Review* titled "Why Socialism?"—an obvious reply by implication to Freud's "Why War?"[18] In this article, Einstein argued for the desirability of a rational socialist order to resolve the basic human problems that capitalist societies were incapable of resolving. He did not directly comment on Freud's theory. Rather, he closely followed Marx's labor theory of value in his economic argumentation for the superiority of socialism over capitalism. It was clear that Einstein was not convinced that a supposedly innate human irrationality would preclude constructing a better social order. In embracing the conclusion that humans had the capability to reform their societies for the better, he essentially endorsed the common Enlightenment rationalist assumptions of both revolutionary and reformist nineteenth-century social theories, which influenced the development of twentieth-century social policy, especially in Europe.

4

Marx, Durkheim, and the Limits of Laissez-Faire Capitalism

The nineteenth-century social theories of Karl Marx and Emile Durkheim prefigured the parameters of contemporary social policy and the welfare state. In separate ways they demonstrated how purely unregulated laissez-faire capitalism would be inimical to human welfare and produce social crises that could ultimately undermine the system itself. Both provided concepts for humanizing societies that have been incorporated, consciously or not, as theoretical underpinnings of contemporary social policy.

Marx's theory, as well as conclusions, began with the nature of capitalism, the subject of the greatest number of his studies. He concluded that market-oriented commodity production determined the internal logic of capitalist development. As capitalism developed, market conditions rather than human needs increasingly dictated living conditions and ways of life. By implication, only a nonmarket-oriented counterlogic would be capable of directly satisfying human needs, one that resulted in some degree of decommodification, and only a radical socialist transformation would be capable of fully making those needs primary. A century and a half later, decommodification has become a central concept in studies of social policy.[1]

Durkheim, unlike Marx, explicitly sought to reform capitalism in order to make it function better. Like Marx, he saw a pure laissez-faire capitalism as producing social breakdowns. But unlike Marx, who saw the breakdown—in the form of class conflict and struggle—as the precursor to progressive change toward the needed socialism, Durkheim saw it as a condition to be avoided and prevented by conscious social planning.

The result of such conscious planning, for which the state was the most appropriate agency, would be social solidarity rather than class conflict.

MARX AND THE LOGIC OF COMMODIFICATION

Marx's focus in *Capital* and elsewhere on the defining importance of the commodity derives from an observation: the feature of capitalism that differentiates it from all previous societies is the pervasiveness of exchanges.[2] Goods and money change hands with a frequency never before encountered in history. The process of buying and selling even extends to the buying and selling of human beings, not just in the sense of past slavery, but also in the current sense of free workers who must sell their mental and physical energies for work to employers through labor markets. The units of exchange—commodities—include goods, money, and human labor.

Commodities are the economic cells of capitalism. The logic of commodity exchange and production—the internal logical of capitalism—is fundamentally different from what existed in previous economic systems. Precapitalist societies produced primarily goods that were directly consumed by their producers rather than, as in capitalist societies, goods that are transformed into commodities to be sold through market transactions to others. The direct goal of most precapitalist production was to produce something useful for the maker's own consumption. A medieval peasant grew potatoes in order to have something to eat. Commodity production, though, could exist in precapitalist societies as when otherwise autarkic peasants took excess crops to intermittent markets for sale.

In the commodity production that characterizes capitalist societies, the primary goal has shifted from producing something useful for self-consumption to producing something from which profits can be derived in its market sale to others. Capitalist farmers grow potatoes in the hopes that they will gain good profits from their sale. What then makes something a commodity is not what it materially is but rather what is done with it. A potato is or is not a commodity depending upon whether it is sold or consumed by its producer.

The great dividing line between precapitalist and capitalist production is that in the former, producer and consumer are one and the same, while in the latter they are different, with the market mediating their relationship and thereby increasingly mediating all human relationships. Producers exchange through market transactions their produced goods—thereby making them into commodities—to others who may or may not be the ultimate consumers depending upon whether they consume or resell the new commodities.

The transformation of goods into commodities is the first step toward constructing a wider and wider net of economic transactions that will tie more and more people together. This is a progressive historical development to the extent that it breaks through the limits of localized production and ties more people together in abstractly cooperative relations. The diets of potato farmers can become more varied as they are able to trade for foods that they themselves cannot produce. The potato and, say, avocado farmers become mutually interdependent as opposed to isolated. The web of economic interrelationships increases, and that very increase expands production possibilities and new forces of production, according to Marx.

The possibility of selling their crops to others through market transactions allows farmers to specialize. The potato peasant was forced to be an all-around producer. The farmer and household members could not live on potatoes alone. They had to supplement that diet by growing their own vegetables and breeding some animals. Commodity-producing potato farmers were able to specialize in growing potatoes because, with the money gained from sales, they could now purchase vegetables and meat produced by others. By specializing they were able to become better producers of potatoes, and thus overall societal production increased. Increasing specialization in that sense increases forces of production.

So far the transformation from goods to commodity production is progressive in terms of increasing production capabilities of societies, and taken alone it could be a justification for free trade, globalization, and a number of other contemporary capitalist developments tied to increasing commerce.

But there are limits to commodification as a progressive force. Extreme unregulated commodification, like overindulgence in food and drink, results in human harm. To understand the limits of commodification as a progressive historical force as Marx did, it is necessary to examine his theory of economic value. Basing himself initially on a distinction made by Aristotle, he found two types of value: use and exchange. Use value is the importance that any good has for the person as she is consuming it. The use value of a potato is that it provides nourishment, has a pleasant taste, and so forth. The primary goal of most forms of precapitalist production was to produce goods that were useful, that is, that had use values. Exchange value is the relative worth of a commodity in a market transaction. A potato costs fifty cents, whereas an avocado costs a dollar. The avocado therefore has twice as much exchange value as the potato. Whether it has twice as much use value in consumption is another matter. What counts is that the primary goal of capitalist production is to produce commodities that are exchangeable at a profit, that is, have exchange value.

Therein lies the rub and flaw in the system: The primary goal of capitalists is to produce commodities from which they can reap profits rather than to produce goods that are useful to society. If a society needs something that would be useful but it cannot be produced at a profit, it will not be produced under pure laissez-faire conditions. Public libraries would not exist if they were required to turn profits. Conversely, if a commodity that is absolutely harmful to society can be produced at a profit, it will be produced. Cigarettes are an obvious example. For sure it is not a stark conflict. Many, perhaps most, commodities also turn out to be useful. A corporate farm–produced potato still provides nourishment and taste, though it is also true that extreme corporate profit maximization can resort to production techniques that diminish that potato's nourishment and taste.

Marx chose not to exploit the conflict between use and exchange value, perhaps because he thought it to be too obvious a flaw in the system. But it is precisely that contradiction that highlights the limitations of the system and has the potential for indicating where reforms, if not revolutionary changes, need to be made. Reforms, at the least, are needed to the extent that the system either does not produce needed goods and services or produces harmful goods and services.

If there is a contradiction between production for usefulness and production for profit, there is by implication also a contradiction between distribution of goods according to need and unregulated market distribution of commodified goods according to the purchasing abilities of consumers. A woman with several children to care for will need a larger house more than will a single male. If, however, the woman has less income than needed to afford the house, whereas the male has enough income, it will be the purchasing ability of the male, not the need of the woman, that will dictate who gets the house. The logic of commodity production according to profit rather than usefulness has its parallel in the logic of commodity distribution according to purchasing power rather than need.

The act of commodity consumption, like the act of commodity production, is thus an alienated act. What dictates consumption is not human need alone but also possession of money—the symbolic form of commodity value. In laissez-faire capitalist conditions, a hurt or sick person, instead of directly being able to seek medical care, must first worry about being able to afford the care. The poorer consumers are, the more they must make the alienated, stressful calculation of whether they can afford to satisfy the need.

What is particularly insidious is that it is an alienation of men and women's own making. They produce the commodities, yet as in Mary Shelley's *Frankenstein*, they produce something that will come back to subtly or not-so-subtly control and, in extreme cases, destroy them.

Market conditions—the semi-autonomous logic of commodity inter-relationships—act as an alien force that controls and constrains how people work and consume, and in many cases whether they are able to work and consume at all. That is because it indeed is an alien force dictating their lives.

But it is humans themselves who have created the force. The market, demystified of all its seeming externality, is simply a grand product of one way that humans produce and consume. There is nothing natural about it. It is not a force of nature. It becomes a force only because humans allow it to become one that controls how they interrelate.

Marx speaks of a fetishism of commodities to capture this dimension of alienation. To make the point, he resorts to the analogy of religious beliefs. From his admittedly atheistic perspective, human beings create beliefs in God or gods. Yet they then believe their mental creations to be independent forces controlling their lives.[3] It is the same with commodities and the market. They are human creations that humans then believe to be independent forces controlling their lives. True consciousness, in Marx's way of inverting the Hegelian dialectic, would require breaking the bonds of alienated religious and market superstitions.

Where this analysis becomes directly relevant to contemporary social policy is that distribution according to purchasing power—or, in more technical economic terms, effective demand rather than need—results in excluding some part of the population from needed goods and services, including basic essentials such as food, housing, and medical care. It follows that any social policy that wishes to ensure that at least minimal subsistence necessities are available to all citizens must counteract the market's innate tendencies for distributing goods and services. There is no profitable way to produce and distribute all necessities for the poor, who are themselves a product of the competitive labor-market struggle within capitalist societies.

Implied in Marx's analysis is that the state is the agency most able to act as a counterforce to the market to distribute goods and services according to need rather than effective demand. It has the capacity through taxation to control sources of revenue, which it can transform into needed goods and services for portions of the population that could not otherwise obtain them. This implication is the basis of all contemporary welfare economics.

Put more abstractly and generally, if commodification goes hand in hand with pure capitalist development, then by implication, decommodification would have to be employed in any effort to humanize society. Full decommodification though, in Marx's revolutionary view, could only be realized with a structural change from capitalism to socialism.

If socialism was the progressive next step in human development, left somewhat ambiguous by Marx was how that step would be taken. Would it be taken all at once, with a sweeping ending of capitalist commodification and an immediate all-round construction of socialist decommodification? Or could it be taken incrementally, with socialist reform measures employed within the contexts of existing capitalist societies? That was the crux of the debate between revolutionary and evolutionary socialists. Marx's own views on the question remained undeveloped. In his most relevant writing, "The Critique of the Gotha Program," he seemed to argue for revolutionary political change but then, once state power was secured, incremental measures to develop actual socialism. In whichever guise, revolutionary or reformist, communist or social democratic, within a socialist country or within a mixed structure, Marx's legacy for social policy was the insight that decommodification had to be a component part of any effective social policy.[4]

DURKHEIM AND SOCIAL SOLIDARITY

Emile Durkheim came of age in the aftermath of the Paris Commune, an event that sent shock waves through French social thinking. On March 18, 1871, with invading German troops occupying France, Parisians, dissatisfied with how their government had conducted the war, rose up and seized control of the city. A week later they declared the city to be an independent commune and elected a governing council that included radical republicans and socialists. The French national government regrouped its forces with the cooperation of German chancellor Bismarck, who released prisoners of war. In May, the French army brutally retook the city from the Communards in street-by-street fighting. Over twenty thousand lives were lost.

While Marx and other socialists saw the uprising as growing out of class struggle and portending socialist revolution, conservatives and liberals like Durkheim saw it as representing an abhorrent breakdown of internal social order in France that should be avoided in the future. Durkheim's general theory should be understood in that context and with those motives. It was both an alternative to Marx's analysis of capitalism and a prescriptive theory to orient social policies so as to promote social order and prevent critical social breakdowns like the Paris Commune.

In the general theory, most represented in *The Division of Labor in Society*, Durkheim rarely used the term *capitalism*. Whereas Marx wrote in terms of feudalism, capitalism, and socialism as the past, present, and future, Durkheim wrote in terms of societies developing from having simple to complex divisions of labor.

What was most revealing about the capitalism of his time for him was not that it was based on private ownership of the means of production and on the production of commodities, but rather that it was a system that was able to coordinate the labors of individuals occupying very different occupational and class positions. Unlike the preceding medieval period when there were few occupational specializations beyond that of peasant, developed capitalism was an enormously complex and complicated affair. It was that very complexity that produced its social superiority over preceding societies, because it created a basis for social order through interdependence. Each occupational specialization and vertical class role was part of one overall interdependent, integrated system in which each needed the other.

His emphases on social interdependence and integration were consistent with his functionalist approach to sociology. He saw social bodies as operating like human bodies, with each part playing a role in maintaining overall health. If the heart plays the role of pumping blood throughout the human body, the family can be seen as playing the role of raising children for the social body. Each part thus fulfills a need that the overall social body has for its survival. What is more, for the social body to function well, each of the parts must play its role well in harmony with the other parts. Put differently, the parts must be integrated into the social body.

If the social body is operating in a healthy manner, each person will feel important and content from performing her or his role well and will feel solidarity with others who are performing their own roles. The sense of solidarity will derive from all of the roles being interdependent and mutually beneficial. Farmers thrive when they have urban markets to sell to; urban people are able to perform urban occupations because farmers sell them the food they need for nutritional sustenance.

Durkheim's functionalism was a modern and secular version of the assumptions of organic and celestial order that had formed the social thinking of Augustine of Hippo in the fourth century. Both approaches stressed the naturalness of hierarchy and order, though Durkheim's approach limited itself to worldly relations. That of Augustine was God ordained. That of Durkheim resulted from the logic of the division of labor.

Modern societies with complex divisions of labor thus provide the initial bases for social order and integration in Durkheim's view. But he did not believe that social order and integration occur automatically. The system is not self-regulating with a natural tendency toward equilibrium, as laissez-faire proponents held. The parts can be badly coordinated and operate at cross-purposes. Incompetent individuals can fill the roles.

In order for a society to function well, its state has to oversee and regulate the division of labor—the true purpose and function of the state, according to Durkheim. In particular, it has to engage in planning, and it has to design and institutionalize mechanisms so that the parts of the division of labor will be filled with the most appropriate persons.

Social order and stability, according to Durkheim, are necessary not only for the social system as a whole but also for individuals within it. One of his great insights was that individuals function better when their social conditions are well structured and relatively predictable. When people can know with relative certainty what to expect, they can plan accordingly. But when the structures to which people are accustomed sharply change or disappear, as they often do in capitalist development, they have a hard time adapting to the new conditions. It is an adaptation process that can be exceedingly stressful and result in physical and mental illness, and in extreme cases, suicide. Durkheim used the term *anomie* to describe this condition of destructuralization and its negative results. For that reason he advocated that social changes occur gradually and not be abrupt and jarring. He in turn believed that governments should assume responsibility for guiding social changes so that they would not produce anomic results.

The backdrop for Durkheim's concern was that the more modern societies have become, the more rapid the rate of technological and social change has been. In the tenth century, not much changed either technologically or socially during the course of a life span. Durkheim, living at the end of the nineteenth century, could see the enormous changes wrought in working and living conditions by industrialization in that century, changes that severely disrupted accustomed ways of life. The pace of technological and social change would accelerate even faster during the next century.

Contemporary complex capitalism, then, is capable of being the basis for a well-integrated social order characterized by social solidarity rather than class conflict, but only so long as the state judiciously regulates the interaction of the roles and the rate of change in the interests of the society as a whole.

Durkheim's legacy for contemporary social policy was to develop a reformist concept of social solidarity distinct from the revolutionary concept of class solidarity associated with left-wing working-class movements. Instead of solidarity being how workers viewed and felt about each other as they engaged in a common struggle against the class enemy, in Durkheim's hands it became a concept that cut across class lines to unite all members of society regardless of class position. If the revolutionary concept of solidarity grew out of class conflict, the Durkheimian concept of solidarity muted the class conflict. The revolutionary concept assumed solidarity among class equals; the Durkheimian concept assumed a societal solidarity that included class unequals. His reformist concept of solidarity would influence the development of the contemporary social policy concepts of solidarity, social cohesion, and social inclusion.

A century later, social policy in Europe has explicitly stated, as central goals, the production of social solidarity and the associated conditions of social integration and inclusion. In the same way that the social breakdowns associated with the Paris Commune propelled the development of Durkheim's original social order theory, the severe breakdown of order caused by World War II propelled the development of the European Union, with its own ambitious prescriptions for social harmony and order.

The concepts of social cohesion, social solidarity, inclusion and social integration, and the welfare state all grow out of social policy attempts to prevent social disorder in and between nations. Therein lies their appeal to European conservatives and liberals. Socialists see in them socialist measures to temper the worst consequences of laissez-faire capitalism.

5

From Theory to Ideology

If social theorists such as Marx and Durkheim provided ideas and concepts that were potentially relevant to social policy development, political ideologists—most prominently conservatives, liberals, and socialists in Europe and the United States—took those ideas and remolded them to guide the actions of political parties and organizations. Political ideology is an intervening step between generalized theoretical, philosophical, and value premises and actual social policy formulation and adoption.

Marx provided ideas that would become cornerstones of twentieth-century socialist and communist ideologies. His influence on other ideologies would be in terms of the fundamental questions he posed about capitalism. The influence of Durkheim was different. He was not a world historical figure like Marx, in whose name political movements and revolutions would be launched. Rather, he was a theorist symptomatic of the turn-of-the-century liberal transformation from acceptance to rejection of laissez-faire capitalism. While there are sociologists who describe themselves as Durkheimians, there are no political actors or movements who describe themselves as such.

Marx's theory had direct political purposes and implications. It was meant to provide tools to socialist and communist parties in their struggles to attain and maintain state power. Durkheim the neopositivist, on the other hand, shied away from describing his mission as directly political. He saw state administration as a kind of straightforward technocratic exercise that should be based upon noncontroversial social scientific knowledge. Nevertheless, his approach provided a theoretical grounding most directly to political liberalism, in that it demonstrated the necessity of state regulation to guide positive economic and social development. His prescriptions for social integration would also unintentionally provide a meeting ground for European conservative, liberal, and social democratic approaches to social policy. In addition to justifying the liberal concern for developing a state-regulated capitalism, Durkheim's ideas addressed the conservative concern for maintaining social order and the traditional community, and the social democratic need to advance incrementally socialistic reforms by creating mixed public-private economic structures that could be seen as significant steps toward a future all-around socialism.

Marx and Durkheim's theories entered into the modern ideological approaches to social problems and social policy that arose in the nineteenth century in reaction to three tectonic shifts: the technological shift from agricultural to industrial societies, the consolidation of economic capitalism and the progressive retreat of feudal remnants, and the beginning shift from autocratic to democratic control of governments.

These massive shifts created new types of social problems and unleashed flurries of political debates about how best to approach understanding and fixing these problems. The shift away from agriculture brought about cities and a host of urban problems. The consolidation of economic capitalism brought about new forms of class conflict. Democratization of governance brought ordinary people into the political arena of ideological struggles.

By the end of the century, the basic outlines of socialist, liberal, and conservative ideological approaches to resolving social problems had emerged, outlines that have held until today.

SOCIALISM

Socialism represented the most radical approach to the social problems of the nineteenth century—poverty, factory exploitation, urban sprawl, rural decline, and family uprooting, among others. Marxian and non-Marxian socialists alike, beginning in the 1840s, concluded that the capitalist system itself was to blame for the problems and that only a new socialist system based upon public ownership of factories, banks, large stores, and other means of producing wealth would be capable of resolving them. They argued that in capitalist societies private owners sought to maximize their individual wealth, resulting in a competitive struggle of all against all, with winners and losers and heightened inequality. In socialist societies, with public ownership and rational planning, industry would be oriented to the good of all of society and would facilitate the achievement of an all-around social equality.

Socialist parties began to develop in Germany (1875), Holland (1877), Belgium (1885), Britain (1893), and Russia (1898), often in conditions of illegality. By the onset of World War I, they had achieved significant representation in a number of European parliaments. Socialist parties, beginning with the Socialist Labor Party in 1898, also formed during this period on American soil and initially had some electoral success, though not as much as in Europe.

World War I produced deep strains within and between parties over whether the war should be supported in the name of patriotism or opposed in the name of working-class internationalism. Many of the major parties endorsed the former position, while V. I. Lenin, Rosa Luxembourg, and the American socialist leader Eugene V. Debs opposed the war.

The 1917 Bolshevik Revolution delivered the fatal blow to socialist unity. In 1919, Lenin called for communists to leave existing socialist parties and create their own parties. The early 1920s then saw the creation of the major western communist parties, with socialism as a movement now divided between communists and socialists.

The two different parties agreed that socialism needed to replace capitalism, but they disagreed on how to attain that goal. Communists believed that a revolutionary overthrow of the capitalist state was necessary, which would then allow for sweeping socialization of the means of production. Socialists argued that it was possible and desirable, because of newly achieved democratic provisions within existing capitalist states, to gain greater and greater control over the state and then institute socialist reforms that would gradually transform the society from capitalist to socialist.

Socialism in whichever guise—communist or social democratic—had a much greater impact on the development of social policy in Europe than in the United States, where a strong socialist tradition did not take root because of the structure of the electoral system and because of general cultural and historical conditions. That is one of the major reasons why American social policy is so much weaker.

LIBERALISM

Nineteenth-century liberals originally championed the capitalistic notions of individual freedom and laissez-faire economics. Adam Smith in 1776, the same year as the American Declaration of Independence, published *The Wealth of Nations* in which he argued that capitalist economies functioned best if the laws of free competition were maintained. Early nineteenth-century liberal economic doctrine, following Smith, argued strongly against government economic interference in the market, which had up to then been in the form of monopolistic privileges granted to aristocracies and court favorites. By the twentieth century, though, one school of liberalism began to see the limits of laissez-faire economics. Unregulated capitalism was producing extremes of inequality and worsening the situation of the poor. Liberals then began to advocate state-regulated capitalism in place of laissez-faire capitalism.[1]

English economist John Maynard Keynes provided the theoretical foundations of twentieth-century economic liberalism, as Durkheim had for turn-of-the-century social liberalism. Keynes concluded that unregulated laissez-faire capitalism would produce a situation in which increasing sectors of the population would be impoverished. Aside from the moral issues involved, such a consequence would eventually destroy the capitalist system. In his *General Theory of Employment, Interest and Money*, Keynes broke with classical economic theorist Jean Baptiste Say's conclusion that supply creates its own demand, that is, that the capitalist economy naturally tends toward equilibrium between the supply of commodities and the demand for them, which was the rationale for the laissez-faire theory that the state should stay out of the economy. Keynes argued that the general equilibrium of the system is compatible with high unemployment, which results in lowering effective demand and causes recession. He explained the old problem of overproduction—which figured prominently in Marx and Engel's *Communist Manifesto* as a potentially fatal flaw in the system—as resulting from a lack of effective demand. The state can re-equilibrate the system through either making public investments or redistributing income for private consumption. The development of efficient social programs, such as health care and education, that can deliver services to the population at lower costs than private businesses can, results in the lower classes having more money to spend on other commodities, thereby increasing the effective demand for them. The state can also increase effective demand by using progressive taxation to redistribute some income downward.

CONSERVATISM

All historical forms of conservatism base themselves on one or another agency of stationary inevitability—God, nature, land, or the market—which are seen as inevitable forces that humans should not attempt to alter.

The word *conservative* first came into use in the early to mid-nineteenth century in reaction to political reforms associated with the French Revolution. Edmund Burke argued, as noted above, that because traditional institutions represented the wisdom of the ages, revolutionary reforms would destroy what the generations had accomplished.[2] As observed by Gerth and Mills, there previously had been no need for an explicitly conservative ideology when medieval traditional assumptions were universally taken for granted. It was only when Enlightenment thinkers broke out of the mold of those assumptions and threatened the prevailing ideological order that what had been taken for granted had to be expressly formulated.[3]

In its first stage, conservative doctrine defended traditional political privileges of kings, aristocracies, and landowners at a time when industrial capitalist interests were seeking to consolidate their economic power with political control of government policies. Conservatives represented a semi-feudal reaction against the increasing market character of societies. At the same time, though, conservatives continued to embrace the medieval feudal concept of noblesse oblige—nobility has obligations, including to the poor. They argued that the well-off had a duty to care for the poor and sponsored much humanitarian legislation.

Karl Mannheim noted that the conservative notion of utopia is "from the very beginning embedded in existing reality." The original conservative center of gravity was closeness to the land.[4] To an important extent, conservatives resisted capitalist transformations that would upset traditional land-based relations. That meaning of conservatism has continued in parts of Europe. But by the twentieth century in the United States, in conformity with the declining relative importance of the agrarian sector, closeness to the capitalist market replaced closeness to the land, with conservatives defending the existing capitalist reality against liberal and socialist-type reforms.

Contemporary conservatism in the United States has taken over the laissez-faire position originally associated with mid-nineteenth-century liberals. Today's conservative in the United States is in essence yesterday's liberal.[5] The free market, according to these conservatives, will ultimately provide solutions for social problems. If individuals and families are required to compete for their survival in market conditions, they will develop self-reliance as character traits. That will serve them better than a mentality of dependence on social welfare programs.

IDEOLOGY AND CULTURE

Contemporary conservatism, liberalism, and socialism in their economic meanings all revolve around the issue of where to set the balance between state and private control of the economy. As total political ideologies, though, they are not restricted as to where to set that balance. They also possess different orientations toward the balance between state and private control of social and cultural matters. Does the state, representing in theory the general will and common good, have any right to impose itself over contrary private social and cultural decisions and activities? Should the state be able to govern the limits of free speech? Should it be able to prohibit the use of profanity on the public airways? Should it be able to govern whether a woman has an abortion? Should it be able to prohibit certain types of aberrant sexual relationships?

In seeming paradoxes, contemporary liberalism endorses state intervention on economic but not cultural matters, while conservatives endorse state intervention on cultural but not economic matters. Liberalism since the nineteenth century has consistently advocated maximizing individual rights and minimizing state interference, unlike its interventionist position on state economic regulation. Conservatism has been less willing to maximize individual rights when they run contrary to traditional norms. While contemporary conservatives in the United States seek to minimize the state's control over economic matters, they seek to at least maintain and sometimes increase its control over social and cultural matters.

Because of these inconsistencies, it is not unusual to find persons who are ideological hybrids. They have one orientation toward economic matters and another toward social and cultural ones. Some can be conservative regarding economic questions and liberal on social and cultural ones—embracing deregulation of industry as well as a woman's right to choose an abortion, for example. Others can have the reverse position of being liberal on economic questions and conservative on social and cultural ones—for instance, embracing progressive taxation and government censorship of profanity on the airways.

Socialists can also be inconsistent. While they consistently advocate the necessity of state economic regulation and control, they are more likely to embrace a liberal attitude toward social and cultural questions.

Communists and libertarians hold the most ideologically consistent polar positions. Communists, at least in the past, have embraced state regulation of social and cultural as well as economic areas, while libertarians have a laissez-faire attitude toward all areas.

CONSERVATIVE COUNTERREFORMS

Since 1980, initially associated with the Reagan and Thatcher governments in the United States and the United Kingdom, the conservative ideological offensive put liberals and socialists on the defensive. Conservatives put forth a renewed, near-fundamentalist faith in laissez-faire capitalism that justified cutbacks in domestic social programs. After the 1989 collapse of the Eastern and Central European communist countries, conservative policy held sway in an aggressive restructuring of the world economy with free trade and privatization of state industries.

In response to this successful conservative onslaught, European socialists retreated from advocating the construction of new socialist economies to defending existing welfare-state programs. The classic socialist ideology that called for building a new economic structure through socialization of the means of production is no longer a part of socialist platforms. At most, today's mainstream socialist parties content themselves with proposing partially socialist solutions to capitalist problems while maintaining a nominal adherence to the classic socialist value of equality.[6]

Liberals in the United States have become so defensive that they rarely publicly identify themselves as liberals. In political discourse, conservatives have successfully transformed *liberal* and *liberalism* into pejoratives that they freely use to tarnish opponents to their ideological left.[7] The belief, held by conservatives and liberals alike, is that substantial portions of the public now have a Pavlovian negative reaction to the words in the same way that previous generations of Americans were brought up on steady diets of anticommunism.

If conservatives have renewed ideological confidence, liberals and socialists have fallen into a kind of ideological disorientation and anomie. In extremes, the anomie is characterized by having no program to offer to the public other than that of being vaguely different from the conservatives. The way out of the anomie will require developing and defending with clarity social reforms that advance traditional liberal and socialist values of equality and solidarity over laissez-faire policies and values of inequality and individualism.

With the ending of the Cold War, the fundamental issue of western politics has shifted from capitalism versus socialism to a struggle between varieties of capitalism. At one pole stands savage capitalism in which inequality and individualism are maximized; at the other pole stands a more humane capitalism in which state programs based on the traditional socialist values of equality and solidarity are used to temper the market's inherent tendencies to produce inequality and poverty. At the core of this struggle, whether explicitly recognized or not, is the issue of free-market versus welfare-state capitalism, American versus European capitalism, weak versus strong social policy.

6

The Origins of Social Policy in Europe and the United States

A ttempts to pin down an exact and satisfying definition of social policy are frustrating. Generically, a social policy is a plan of action for addressing a particular social problem, while the grand set of social policies within a society constitutes its overall social policy. In practice, though, contemporary social policy analysts do not take up all possible social problems. Most, for example, consider crime, despite its falling within the broad definitions of a social problem, to be a separate issue to be addressed by legal and criminal justice policies. On the other hand, high rates of crime can be legitimately taken as in large measure indicating failures of social policy, as we will discuss in chapter 14.

To a large extent the field of contemporary social policy turns out to be tautologically what its analysts consider it to be: primarily plans of action that address such core social welfare problems and issues as inequality, poverty, unemployment, health care provision, family support, and racial and ethnic issues.

Social policy is often identified with the modern welfare state. But they are distinct concepts. A social policy is a plan of action for dealing with a particular social problem. A welfare state is a state that takes on as a central task assuring the overall well-being of its citizens. Before the 1930s, a number of governments had limited social policies to deal with particular social problems, but no government took on as a central task constructing an overall welfare state to assure the well-being of its citizens.[1] States mainly committed themselves to maintaining public order and defending citizens in case of war. The British government first used the term *welfare state* during World War II to mobilize its citizens in the struggle against the Nazis.[2]

The basic assumption of social policy is that the normal workings of the economy of any society cannot be counted upon to produce complete human welfare, however that is defined, for its members. Those who are able to participate in production and receive normal levels of income will have the means to be able to enjoy at least average well-being. But those who are unable to participate in economic production (the young, the infirm, the old, the unemployed) and those who are at a disadvantage in economic distribution (minimum-wage workers, for example) will not have their welfare needs covered unless there are countervailing social policy measures to distribute some part of the overall economic product according to need.

ORIGINS OF SOCIAL POLICY

Social policy, whether reflected upon with intention or not, has been a part of every human community in history. In the earliest hunting-and-gathering societies, adults provided food, shelter, and other needs to children who would have otherwise starved, since they were too young to be able to produce for themselves. Those societies could not have survived if only direct producers were able to consume goods and services. There would have been no children able to survive and become the new societal members of the future. Those societies had to have implicit social policies of distributing some part of goods and services according to need rather than success in production.

As societies grew larger and more complex, clans, families, and households became more distinguishable from the communal wholes and took direct responsibility for the welfare of their members. For most societies, it is the family—not the communal society as a whole, as in the hunting-and-gathering period—that is thought of as the originator of welfare provision, and indeed it continues to be a pillar of welfare provision today. Families generally provide for their children according to their needs rather than their productive contributions.

As societies grew still larger and more complex, individuals in need who were not attached to particular households, families, or clans increased. So too did whole families and households in need. That created a new population in need that required two new forms of welfare provision: charitable contributions from individuals and churches and relief from states. The Roman state, as early as 123 BC, subsidized the sale of grain so that the poor could afford to purchase it.[3]

From the Roman period until relatively recently, the family, charity, and the state, in that order, have been the forms through which welfare provision according to need rather than productive contribution have flowed. In the middle of the nineteenth century in the most prosperous European and North American countries, states became more aggressive actors in welfare provision, both because of the inadequacy of the family and charity forms and because they now had the capacity to do so, resulting from increasing tax revenues fueled by long-term economic growth.

Modern social and welfare policy starts, like all social and welfare policies, with the reality that the normal workings of the economy are insufficient to meet the needs of all members of the population. It distinguishes between the welfare that can be provided by the normal workings of the economy and that which must be supplemented by the family, the state, and charity. Every modern welfare system and the social policy guiding it contain a mix of these. But how they are mixed differs greatly.

In very general terms, American social policy attempts to minimize supplementary state participation in welfare delivery, while European policies rely more on the state. The actual amounts spent on welfare are not greatly different. What is different is how they are spent and what the outcomes are.[4] Related to the different approaches are different attitudes toward decommodification and social inclusion, the issues originally raised by Marx and Durkheim.

EUROPE

Despite Europe comprising a number of countries with separate social policies, there have been common seminal developments and a confluence of economic, historical, and cultural contexts. European capitalism developed first as a marginal feature of the otherwise fully feudal Middle Ages. As the market system grew stronger, it provoked a protracted, centuries-long struggle with feudal traditionalism, a struggle that involved both the ability of markets to expand and which sets of economic interests states would represent. Contemporary European capitalism is the outgrowth of this struggle.

While feudalism was vanquished, the influence of its challenge helped to shape the form that European capitalism took. Catholicism, the monopoly religion of feudalism, has continued to exercise strong cultural influence down to the present. Its key doctrines on the role of the family and view of the poor determined some of the ways in which social policies developed.

Also important is that socialist and communist political movements and parties, in part spawned by the influence of the French Revolution, grew to significance in Europe. Socialism and communism became important ideological forces that either provided elements of social policy development or required compromises from more conservative forces.

In the 1880s, conservative chancellor Bismarck pioneered modern social insurance with programs to protect workers against sickness, old age, and injury, in part to counter the rising influence of the socialist labor movement in Germany. The initial benefits were low, though, and did not cover all workers.

The next seminal event in European welfare-state development came with World War II and its aftermath. In the United Kingdom, the Beveridge Report, released during the war in 1942, put forth the need to develop a comprehensive welfare state in the postwar period that would protect workers against sickness, old age, and other problems. In 1946, just after the war, the Labour government launched the National Health Service, which guaranteed as a social right access to health care for all citizens.

The postwar period saw a quantum leap in the development of European welfare states, with all countries developing universal health insurance and a large number of other publicly financed social programs. Part of the motives grew from national cultural traditions that sought to develop interclass solidarity among their citizens. Others were more directly in response to domestic and regional leftist pressures. Communist parties had played a major role in leading resistance organizations within the Nazi-occupied countries and were poised to parlay that prestige into political clout in the postwar period. As Eastern and Central Europe came under Soviet and communist domination and developed comprehensive welfare states, the Western European countries developed their own versions so as not to be perceived as socially inferior in the eyes of their own working classes.

The founding of the European Union in 1993 culminated nearly a half-century of preliminary moves toward continental integration—both to increase the economic power of Europe in the world economy and to preclude any historical repetition of the national divisions that had resulted in the disastrous experiences of World Wars I and II. The EU moved quickly to expand membership beyond its original Western European member countries to the formerly socialist Central and Eastern European countries, toward the goal of effecting a truly continental integration.

Initial integration goals were economic and political—creating common commodity, labor, and capital markets with a common currency, the Euro, and creating a European parliament with a status of European citizenship that would allow free movement without need of passports across internal borders, as citizens of the United States have in being able to cross state lines. The notion of social integration was not among the original top priorities. That changed at the Lisbon Summit in 2000 when the EU made as an explicit goal increasing the social cohesion of the member states by 2010. Later that year at the Nice Summit, the EU set out a requirement for its member states to develop national action plans to increase social inclusion. It began discussions on adopting a common set of social indicators to measure progress toward attainment of social inclusion within the member countries.

The goal of social inclusion, with its Durkheimian roots, had resurfaced in the 1970s in France and gained currency in European discussions of social policy. As currently formulated, it essentially means that social policy should have a goal of integrating persons into the community and its activities, and of avoiding, eliminating, or at least diminishing existing social practices that lead to social exclusion. That very general policy goal dictates that existing sources of social exclusion must be identified and then policies developed to address them.

The two major sources of social exclusion around which there is a strong European consensus are poverty and unemployment, because both diminish the capabilities of individuals and families to participate fully in their societies. The European Union has thus adopted the goal of eliminating or at least diminishing both. As a result it has a stated goal of diminishing poverty in its member countries by 2010. Farther-ranging discussions address education, discrimination, immigration, and other areas and issues where social exclusion is evident. Common to all is an updated Durkheimian attempt to strengthen the bonds tying individuals together in harmony and solidarity.

As much as Durkheim's original notion of solidarity perpetuated rather than attacked social inequality, to the consternation of the socialists of his time, today's socialists, liberals, and even conservatives in Europe seem to have found common ground with its derived concept of social inclusion. To liberals, social inclusion means integration, to conservatives it means shoring up the traditional community, and to socialists it means combating the atomism and inequality engendered by the market.[5]

THE UNITED STATES

American social welfare developed out of a unique historical and cultural context that was not shared by Europe. This American exceptionalism has become a vital factor in efforts to explain why the United States is indeed different from Europe despite sharing a similar first-world status,[6] and why, in this case, American social policy underdeveloped compared to that of Europe.

Several factors enabled a more laissez-faire capitalist orientation to prevail in the United States, one that would ultimately only begrudgingly allow for any welfare-state development. American capitalist development was unencumbered by a traditional feudal past and unchallenged by strong socialist and communist movements. This gave it, as Lewis Hartz classically noted, largely a tabula rasa or blank sheet to develop upon.[7]

American colonists came from the parts of Europe that were the most capitalistically developed. They carried with them capitalist notions of how to order their economies, and they did not have to confront or compete with absolutist states or state churches for economic control.

American colonists also did not confront dense populations of indigenous persons with noncapitalist institutions. Rather, they confronted sparse populations that would quickly be outnumbered and forced aside. Unlike in the part of North America that would become Mexico, where the colonists never became a majority and were required to use indigenous labor as the base of the economic and social pyramid, American colonists had no need for indigenous labor. All they wanted from the indigenous peoples was their land, which they took violently over the course of three centuries of warfare as they and their capitalistic economies moved westward from the Atlantic to the Pacific.

Capitalism was thus able to develop in a more uncompromised fashion in the United States than in Europe. Competitive market relations were able to more extensively influence social and cultural developments. The logic of the market was a largely unhampered force influencing how the rest of the society developed.[8] Pure capitalist development has thus gone further in the United States than anywhere else. Of course it is still not completely pure, nor will it ever be, but it is purer than elsewhere.

Important also is that it was Protestants, not Catholics as in medieval Europe and Mexico, who established the initial cultural character of the country. It was their institutions and attitudes toward social questions that would greatly influence subsequent social attitudes even when they became secularized. As Max Weber pointed out classically, the Puritans who came to New England carried with them the Calvinist—not Augustinian—interpretation of predestination.[9] Economic success and failure were signs from God indicating salvation or condemnation in the next life. Calvinists and Puritans embraced the work ethic, inherited from Luther's concept of the calling as a self-fulfilling prophecy. Hard work ensured economic success, which was a sign not just of virtue but also of salvation. Whereas the medieval Augustinian-founded Catholic doctrine saw the poor as a part of the organic community to whom the more economically fortunate were obligated to extend charity, the Calvinists saw the poor as deserving their fate because it was predestined by God. This religious view would take the eventual secular form in American cultural development of viewing the poor as undeserving of charity or state aid because their plight was evidence, not of God's disfavor, but of their not having the unchallenged work ethic or other necessary moral qualities.

The history of American social welfare development has thus been burdened by the cultural stigma that poverty carries. The unchallenged and seemingly self-evident cultural value of hard work engenders the parallel assumption that the poor are responsible for causing their own fate and thus are undeserving of help. There is a dominant belief that the United States is a wide-open continent unfettered by feudal institutions or oppressive governments. It is a land of opportunity in which any person willing to work hard can succeed. Failure is a sign of unworthiness, if not in the eyes of God as the Puritans believed, then in the eyes of the hard-working individuals who are responsible for the country's greatness.

Three cultural values of particular importance emerged out of the originating conditions of the United States: individualism, limited egalitarianism, and a suspicion of the state. Individualism was consistent with the values of the Protestant colonists. If Catholicism presented believers with a fully developed ready-made set of group beliefs that they were to unquestionably embrace, Protestantism presented them with a looser outline of beliefs, leaving it up to them individually to complete the belief system. If the Catholic inclination led to dogmatism and group cohesion, the Protestant inclination led to sectarian division and individualism, as Durkheim classically argued.[10]

The frontier character of American development also was responsible for favoring individualism. The original colonists, after all, made conscious decisions to leave the traditional constraints of their preexisting English and European societies to strike out to freely create their own individual conditions of life. And it was the Americans, unlike the Canadians, who chose to reject the constraints of British colonial rule so that they could freely create their own nation. Then, as the nineteenth century progressed, waves of pioneers pushed ever westward in search of their own individual secular salvations.

The ethics of individualism and freedom have been thus deeply embedded in the national culture from the beginning. Individualism and freedom could go further on American soil because, it is true, they were not constrained by oppressive state conditions. But it is also true that they were not constrained by institutionalized group loyalties or responsibilities, and those ethics would develop only weakly in American history.

In part because of the strong commitments to individualistic freedom, Americans have been unusually suspicious of state activities to promote social welfare. They abhor having to pay taxes to support state social programs. Despite paying the lowest tax rates in the developed world, they continually complain that they are being overtaxed. No politician can survive in this climate if he or she advocates raising taxes, especially to support social programs, no matter how necessary it might be.

Americans have been egalitarian, but in a different way than Europeans, and this would affect social policy. Alexis de Tocqueville noted in the 1820s that Americans did not pay as much overt deference to status differences as did Europeans.[11] There was a populist ethic in which every person regardless of wealth was seen as being basically the same. The upper classes in turn have been, despite notable exceptions, relatively constrained against flaunting their privileges as they did during the Gilded Age. But even when the upper classes did flaunt their wealth, that did not necessarily mean that the lower classes acknowledged them as being socially superior.

The American notion of egalitarianism also differs from the European one in that it restricts itself to equality of opportunity, with little concern about equality of outcome. Each person is supposed to have an equal chance to work hard and succeed—key components of the American Dream. The United States, as the slogan goes, is the land of opportunity, with in theory no economic, social, or political obstacles placed in the path of each individual's achievement of success. If, the theory goes, opportunities exist and each person can pursue them equally, then those who fail in this quest have only themselves to blame. There is no obligation for the society as a whole to develop welfare programs to protect them. There is also no obligation for those who succeed far beyond the average to give up any of their excess gains for those who do not succeed, or for the general welfare of the community. It is a contradictory ethic of limited egalitarianism built upon the ethic of individualism.

Opportunity of course has been far from equalized. That dissonant reality is freely acknowledged. At best it leads to liberal calls for renewed efforts to equalize opportunities, primarily through education. It has yet to lead to any substantial national discussion on limiting inequality of outcome.

In sum, because of its unique originating historical conditions, American culture is laced with strong cultural values of individualism, suspicion of state social activities, and limited egalitarianism. These have clearly been inimical to the development of a strong social welfare system. At the same time, these values are by no means universally embraced in the United States. American history has witnessed powerful challenges to them. While it is true that union and socialist movements have not developed as strongly in the United States as in Europe, there have been union and socialist movements nonetheless. While the American social welfare system is relatively underdeveloped, it is not nonexistent. There are components of the American system that are comparable in principle to those in Europe. It would therefore be erroneous to assume that its presently dominant cultural conditions prohibit the United States from ever developing a strong social welfare system.

Structural as well as cultural factors have significantly contributed to the underdevelopment of the American welfare state. Key among these is restrictive labor law. A large part of the reason why there is a lower percentage of union members in the United States than in Europe is that American labor law makes it much more difficult to organize unions. According to a survey administered by Lipset and Meltz, 48.2 percent of nonunion employees in the United States would vote for union representation if they had the chance.[12] That indicates that at least half of American workers either belong to or would like to belong to unions—a figure that would be in line with European union densities if it were as easy to organize and join unions on the American side of the Atlantic. Since unions in Europe and the United States have strongly favored and lobbied for the development of social protections through state social welfare programs, any structural frustration of their ability to organize labor force participants necessarily inhibits the development of a strong social welfare system.

The social welfare system that does exist in the United States developed relatively late compared to those of Europe. There was no comprehensive federal approach to social policy in the United States prior to the 1930s. There were only state and local government-sponsored programs of support for the poor, disabled, widows, orphans, the aged, and the unemployed, and these varied greatly in the amount of relief offered. The one exception to this pattern was military pensions, which the federal government first established for veterans of the War of Independence and later for those of the Civil War.[13]

As the Great Depression of the 1930s developed, resulting in as much as one-third of the work force becoming unemployed and rampant poverty, it became quickly apparent that the traditional forms of relief, including charities and state and local programs, were insufficient.[14] Families could provide for some of their members in difficulties, but most did not have enough resources to cover all of the costs, and there were many individuals who did not have families to fall back upon.

Franklin Delano Roosevelt came into office in 1933 with the country in economic and social crisis. He moved quickly to establish emergency programs in agriculture, industry, and finance to attempt to minimally keep the economy from sinking further and to maximally turn the corner toward recovery. The president aggressively laid to rest, at least for that moment in American political history, two widely held assumptions in American politics: that the federal government had to have a laissez-faire policy toward the economy and that public social policies were primarily in the domain of state, not federal, government.

The capstone of Roosevelt's social policy was the Social Security Act of 1935. It established programs for unemployment insurance, retirement benefits, and direct assistance to various categories of unemployable people, including the blind, widows, orphans, and dependent children.

It was not the great need caused by the Depression that led to New Deal social legislation. Rather, as Piven and Cloward argued persuasively, it was that the victims of the Depression mobilized and put pressure on the system to the point of frightening national elites. There were marches of the unemployed, such as the Bonus March, in which unemployed veterans camped out near the capitol in Washington, DC, and then were violently dispersed by army troops. Many joined socialist and communist parties. Had the poor and unemployed simply sunk deeper in misery and not responded, the system would have continued the same instead of conceding reforms.[15]

The next expansion of the American welfare state came during the Lyndon Baines Johnson administration (1963–1968). Johnson, following upon a thrust first established in the John F. Kennedy administration (1961–1963), declared a war on poverty to be a cornerstone of his domestic policy. Out of his administration came the creation of the Medicare medical insurance program for the aged, the Medicaid medical insurance program for the poor, and a variety of programs aimed at reducing poverty, including the Head Start program, which provides preschool education for poor children. Like the 1930s expansion of social welfare programs, the 1960s expansion was at least in part stimulated by severe social turmoil, including the outbreak of riots in numerous black ghettos.

The subsequent period, especially from the Ronald Reagan administration (1981–1988) forward has seen no further expansions of American welfare programs. The major federal policy debates, consistent with the political ascendance of the conservative wing of the Republican Party, have concerned how to cut back social spending, or at least restructure it. The period of welfare-state retrenchment corresponded with increasing income inequality, stagnation in poverty reduction, and falling real wages for the working class since the early 1970s.

Conservative critics of the welfare state succeeded in moving social policy debates from how to design new programs to resolve problems to how to reduce or eliminate existing ones. They argued that the programs sapped individual initiative and the work ethic, created dependency, and were an unaffordable fiscal drain on the nation. They have had more success in cutting means-tested programs that benefit the poor, such as housing subsidies and Aid to Families with Dependent Children, than programs that have universal benefits, such as Social Security and Medicare, which help middle-class as well as low-income retirees.[16] At the same time, conservatives have attempted to privatize existing programs by, for example, hiring private contractors to administer programs and redesigning Social Security so that a part of the revenues would be diverted into stock-market Individual Retirement Accounts (IRAs).

7

Alternative Approaches to Social Policy

Social policy evolved differently in Europe than in the United States because of a greater willingness to rely upon government to counteract the natural tendencies of unregulated private economies to generate poverty, unemployment, inequality, and other social problems. The laissez-faire approach to social problems favored by the most conservative of American policy makers relies on commodified market solutions and the values of individual responsibility and competitive individualism. Only as a last resort should decommodified nonmarket solutions be employed.

There are degrees of market reliance. The most laissez-faire degree relies completely on market forces to produce human welfare. When labor activists sought to have a Connecticut city adopt a policy that would require town contractors to pay their workers a "living wage" that was above the minimum wage, the leading state newspaper articulated the laissez-faire principle in its editorial opposition: "It is better to let market forces determine how much workers should be paid rather than having a municipality tell businesses what to do."[1] Not discussed was what to do if market forces resulted in wages below the poverty level, creating a population of working poor.

The first fallback line of defense for laissez-faire advocates when market forces prove incapable of producing full human welfare is to use the state to create conditions, such as through its fiscal policy or construction of infrastructure, so that the market can perform better. Rather than a living-wage policy, the city should offer tax breaks to encourage business activity. The next fallback is to provide the working poor with services according to need but use private contractors for their delivery. For example, a city government might purchase food supplements for the poor from private contractors. Only after these measures have proven insufficient should completely nonmarket, decommodified means be reluctantly applied, such as publicly financed and operated supplementary food programs.

What breathes life into the market, according to this approach, are individuals competitively struggling to maximize their personal interests. By implication, individuals have a moral responsibility both to work hard and to competitively struggle against each other in order to achieve market success. Max Weber meets Thomas Hobbes, the work ethic and the struggle of all against all, with each man being the other's wolf. Social good results from this individualistic struggle, as does the maximization of individual interests.

In contrast, state-interventionist approaches to social problems start from the explicit assumption, theoretically articulated by Marx and Durkheim, that the market is inherently incapable of satisfying all economic and social needs.[2] They include as an avowed goal optimizing the social as well as the economic functioning of society. If the laissez-faire approach largely treats social functioning as either a residual effect of economic functioning or as a private sphere not to be interfered with, then the state-interventionist approaches prioritize attention to social functioning via policies aimed at strengthening social inclusion—that is, at ensuring that all citizens have the means to participate in a normal manner in the society.

More proactive, government-based approaches to solving social problems are consistent with the principle of decommodification, defined by Esping-Andersen as "the degree to which individuals, or families, can uphold a socially acceptable standard of living independently of market participation."[3] The more citizens can attain necessary goods and services as social rights rather than by virtue of market performance, the less worrisome, anomic, and stressful their daily lives become. Where decommodification has become most prominent has been in the socialization and thereby equalization of the risks of illness, unemployment, and poverty.[4]

For developed societies, the comprehensiveness of a welfare state that can be afforded depends primarily on the balance it chooses between how much national income to distribute as private disposable income for individuals and families and how much to distribute as social income for all citizens. The more of the latter, the more the decommodification of income. All countries distribute at least some part of their national incomes socially in order to pay for national defense, road construction, and the like. Welfare states distribute income as well for social programs.

Critics argue that welfare states have become unaffordable, especially in today's competitive global economy. This assertion, though, makes a question of relative choice into a seemingly inevitable absolute condition. For developed societies, there is considerable choice over where to set the balance between individual and social income. Even in the worst of situations, when national income is declining, it is still possible to preserve comprehensive welfare states by decreasing private income.

There is thus significant economic latitude over whether to construct or preserve comprehensive welfare states. The question of whether to do so is essentially political, despite welfare-state critics attempting to convince the public that their position has economic inevitability on its side.

SOCIAL POLICY OPTIONS

The opposing American laissez-faire and European state-interventionist models result in different choices, in nature or degree, in how to approach, administer, and finance social programs and benefits, and these choices have different social consequences. These options concern who is responsible for welfare provision, who the providers and beneficiaries should be, how to determine eligibility, how generous benefits should be, and how benefits should be financed.[5]

Responsibility

Underlying a laissez-faire approach is the principle that responsibility for providing welfare resides in individuals and families themselves. They should be self-reliant and not dependent on outsiders for their needs. If extreme individualism contains the negative value of not caring about others, then self-reliance is its justifying virtue of not being a burden on others. Individual and familial responsibilities writ large as societal approaches seek to maximize private wages and incomes and minimize taxes and social programs.

The polar approach, consistent with decommodification, calls for socializing responsibility for welfare provision to the whole society. It is consistent with traditional aristocratic notions of noblesse oblige, Catholic charitable obligations to the poor, and socialist statism. In its modern guise, there is an additional belief that such socialization of responsibility is necessary as well as desirable. It is necessary because individuals and families are increasingly incapable of being fully self-reliant as societies become more interdependent, a point made by Durkheim, among others.[6] It is desirable because it represents the institutionalization of the altruistic value of social solidarity as opposed to the selfish value of individualism.

Providers

Private businesses, families, charities, and the state are all active today as planners and providers of welfare goods and services, but with different motives and structural contexts. For private enterprises, profit is the most important consideration. They can only become providers if it is profitable. But the poor cannot afford to purchase many of the goods and services offered by providers. If the poor were required to purchase their own health care and housing at market rates, most would have to go without. The same structural limitations on the capacity of private enterprises to provide needed goods and services at a profit exist for higher classes as well. Most libraries would have to close if they had to be operated as profit-making private businesses, and the public would have to do without access to them. The same holds for public schools. The actual costs of educating a child are so high that most parents could not afford to pay them if all schools were run as private profit-making businesses. The extent to which private businesses can be effective providers is thus structurally limited by their need to earn profits.

Because not all individuals have the requisite purchasing power to purchase necessities at market rates, a second set of providers that includes families, charities, and the state becomes necessary. These deliver goods and services on the principle of need within an economy that is supplementary or countervailing to the normal profit-based one.

Families and charities distribute according to the principle of need rather than profitability. But it is their own voluntaristic determination of need that decides whether, to whom, and how much to distribute, rather than necessarily the actual needs of all those in need. A family will be much more likely to help its own members than outsiders. A church that embraces opposition to abortion may provide help to have an unwanted baby adopted but not to abort it. A charity may be set up to finance research into a particular disease regardless of whether that disease necessarily affects a great number of people. Diseases that are more damaging may not attract as much interest.

The state or government is able to provide goods and services in ways that private businesses, families, and charities cannot. It can define all members of a society as eligible for needed goods and services. It can prioritize the social problems that it wishes to address. It can distribute goods and services without regard to whether the activity is profitable, though not without disregard to cost.

In between the state and private sector is a hybrid institution—the nonprofit corporation—that in theory provides the virtues of the private corporation's competitiveness without its need to make a profit. Because of this unique combination, nonprofit corporations are supposed to be able to provide welfare goods and services at lower costs and more efficiently than either profit-making businesses or state entities.

But what nonprofits gain in cost efficiency is often at the expense of their labor forces. In order to lower operating costs and improve their competitiveness, managers of the nonprofits typically pay their workers less than what comparable state-sector workers receive.

Eligibility

Governments can design programs that provide benefits only to those directly affected by a particular problem—the means-tested approach; or they can design them to benefit all members of the society—the universal approach. In the former, potential recipients of a benefit must be tested to see if they qualify. If a program is designed to provide food supplements only to the poor, then the recipients must be shown to be demonstrably poor before they can receive the food. On the other hand, national health insurance programs or public education systems, for which all citizens are eligible regardless of income, represent universalistic approaches.

European welfare systems, on balance, have more universal programs than does the U.S. system. For that reason, Europeans identify "welfare" and the "welfare state" with programs that benefit the whole society, whereas Americans tend to identify them with programs that only benefit the poor. Consequently, in Europe, receiving welfare does not carry a social stigma with it, whereas it often does so in the United States. Further, because of the more universalistic nature of European welfare systems, there is more popular support for them, especially when cutbacks are threatened. In the United States, on the contrary, welfare programs have less political and popular support when cutbacks are threatened because they are perceived to benefit only the minority poor.

Corporatist programs are in between the means-tested and universal ones. In corporatist programs, societal members receive benefits according to the contributions they have made—the higher the contributions, the greater the benefits. The Social Security retirement program in the United States, in which the size of retirement benefits depends on the size of contributions over a work life, is an example. Benefits are neither targeted to the most needy nor equally available to all citizens.

Beneficiaries

Benefits can be attainable through the workplace as fringe benefits or to all citizens as rights or entitlements. As in the distinction between means-tested and universal benefits, the issue is whether the program is available to and benefits only a subset of the population—the employed whose pay packages include the benefits in question—or all citizens. The difference is that, in the above, the targeted subset is defined by need—usually means-tested poverty—while here it is defined by having a desirable status, like being employed in a stable position that includes benefits.

From the point of view of liberals and socialists, tying benefits to employment was always a fallback position when benefits could not be attained as state-guaranteed universal rights. From the point of view of conservatives, employment-related benefits represent a compromise. They compromise the positions of pure market dependence and individual responsibility on the one hand with an incentive to find work and perform well in it on the other.

The obvious problem of tying benefits to employment is that it leaves out the unemployed and the employed whose pay packages do not include fringe benefits. One solution to this problem has been to tie benefits to employment for the employed and then have the state provide benefits for the rest.

That solution, though, leaves the benefits vulnerable to the vicissitudes of the market and to employer interests. If it is not legally mandated, employers are at liberty to discontinue the benefits if they become too expensive. A significant number of employers in the United States have responded to the rising cost of health insurance by either eliminating the benefit entirely or by requiring their employees to pay a higher share of the cost.

Comprehensiveness of Benefits

Many programs in principle deliver universal benefits but differ in whether those benefits are sufficient to resolve the problem. A health insurance policy that only offers a 10 percent discount on prescription drugs offers little more than token universal relief. Unemployment insurance that only replaces a small fraction of the former earnings and is of short duration will not fully resolve the resulting problems for the person thrown out of work. An income-tax deduction for child-care expenses has universal applicability and spares families some of the financial burdens, but it is far short of fully subsidizing the cost. In these respects, the European welfare programs in general offer far more generous benefit amounts than do those of the United States.

Financing

Tax-financed social programs differ according to how their costs are distributed among different income groups. The more progressive the tax collection is, the higher the proportion of income that must be paid by higher-income groups compared to lower-income citizens. The more progressive the tax system as the source of income becomes, the more redistributive and egalitarian the effect is in terms of benefit payments. Europe and the United States both have progressive tax systems, but the former's systems are, in general, more progressive, resulting in their welfare systems being more redistributive downward.

COMPARATIVE WELFARE STATES

The two polar types of laissez-faire and state-interventionist approaches to social policy incorporate different visions of how to best structure social relations within societies. The first relies completely on self-reliance, is lodged in the private sector, and has highly unequal results. In the earliest version, families used their own resources to take care of their own. With families having unequal resources, the inevitable result was inequality. In the latest version, individuals and families purchase insurance and old-age annuity products from private corporations. In the case of the earliest version, since purchasing powers are unequal, the resulting protections from sickness costs and income loss due to retirement are highly unequal. When this type of policy must resort to public programs, it attempts to target only the needy for benefits and eschews developing universal entitlement programs.

The second type relies on the socialization of costs and risks, is lodged in the public sector, and has egalitarian results. The state uses progressive taxes to collect revenues according to ability to pay and then distributes benefits according to need. Since benefits are distributed according to need, they are not distributed equally. But since sickness strikes unequally and old age has unequal costs, the effect is to equalize living conditions and is therefore egalitarian.

Laissez-faire and state-interventionist principles orient social policy debates. The more the first principle wins out, the more commodified labor and social life is and the more wages are paid individually. The more the second wins out, the more labor and social life are decommodified and the more labor is paid social wages which include tax-financed social benefits.

These represent polar choices in social policy. Within these polar types there are significant subtypes that are closer to actual national welfare regimes. Within the laissez-faire type, there are conservative and liberal variations, with the United States most closely representing the conservative and the United Kingdom and Canada the liberal. The main difference is the relatively higher number of state-provided social programs and benefits permitted in the latter than in the former.

Within continental Europe, there are corporatist and social democratic variations of the welfare state that are closer to the state-interventionist model.[7] Though they often produce similar results in terms of citizen social welfare, they do so in different ways and are based on different theoretical assumptions, ideological values, and political party proponents.[8]

Social democratic welfare policy, most prominently represented in the Scandinavian countries, developed as a middle way between communist proposals for rapid all-around socialist transformations of societies and laissez-faire proposals to make human welfare completely dependent on market performance. Like the communists, social democrats assumed that societies were composed of classes with competing interests, they embraced social equality as a goal, and they were secular in orientation. But if the communists assumed that class membership was the most important source of identity and interests, the social democrats gave individual identity more importance. If communists assumed that the working class needed only one revolutionary party to represent its interests, thereby justifying a dictatorship of the proletariat, the social democrats embraced political pluralism in which they would contend with other parties for influence over state policy. They sought to use the state to advance socialist goals, including welfare policy, without completely monopolizing it.

The corporatist model, which has been influential especially in Germany, France, and Italy, was originally developed as a Catholic alternative to secular socialist doctrines of either the social democratic or communist variety. Catholic-based Christian democratic parties took an originally medieval, Augustinian-founded Catholic notion that the rich have an obligation to perform good works by, among other acts of charity, giving alms to the poor and institutionalized it into state-welfare policy. Underlying this policy was a view of society as being composed of naturally unequal groups that ought to live in organic harmony.

Unlike the social democrats, there is no explicit goal in the corporatist model of producing social equality. But, at the same time, it also does not represent the extreme Calvinist view that poverty is a sign of God's disfavor, which has been influential in American culture. The poor have a place and right to survive in the Catholic world, thereby justifying welfare programs on their behalf. If the social democrats assume the modernist notion of the individual as the basic unit of society, then traditional Catholic social doctrine places the devout practicing family as the basic unit. It represents, therefore, not the extreme individualism that is most often associated with typical market capitalist values. For Catholic liberals, as pointed out by Teresa Montagut, social harmony is a factor analogous to the social solidarity of the left.[9]

In sum, there are three European social policy models and one American model for confronting the common social problems of inequality, poverty, unemployment, family issues, health care, race and ethnic division, and crime (see table 7.1). Taken together, the European models attack these problems more aggressively than the American model does, and they also have more favorable results, as will be seen in the chapters that follow.

Table 7.1. Conservative, Liberal, Christian Democratic, and Social Democratic Welfare States

	Conservative	*Liberal*	*Christian Democratic*	*Social Democratic*
Representative Countries	United States	United Kingdom	France, Italy, Germany	Sweden, Finland, Norway
View of Class	Organic class harmony	Organic class harmony	Organic class harmony	Class struggle
Unit of Society	family	individual	family	individual
View of Inequality	Inequality as outcome of marketplace is desirable	Extreme inequality as outcome of marketplace is undesirable	Inequality is natural	Equality is a goal
Attitude toward Religion	Religious	Secular	Religious	Secular
Social Benefit Amounts	Low	Medium	Medium	High

8

Social Cohesion
and Inequality

Modern European views of equality and inequality developed initially in reaction to the taken-for-granted inequality of the medieval world. Beginning in the seventeenth century, thinkers such as John Locke began to undermine guiding medieval assumptions of inequality. By the eighteenth century, Enlightenment thinkers attacked legal and political inequality, arguing that all men (and not necessarily women) should be equal before the law and be able to vote for their leaders. That was the foundation for democratic reform.

They did not, though, agree on other aspects of equality: whether humans were equal in terms of natural endowments or whether there should be social equality in terms of distribution of wealth and income. Jean-Jacques Rousseau, for example, while embracing legal and political equality, was careful to add that "the word [*equality*] must not be understood to mean that . . . riches should be equally divided between all."[1]

Prevailing Enlightenment views endorsed, at a minimum, legal and political equality. The law should treat all equally regardless of their stations in life, and each person should be equally represented in governance. The former was in opposition to the medieval practice of only recognizing people of stature as being credible witnesses. The latter was in opposition to the prevailing European practice from the thirteenth to the eighteenth centuries of kings gathering advisory bodies—the estates—made up respectively of representatives of the nobility, clergy, and commons (townspeople of substance such as shop owners). Peasants were not represented, or at best the rural-based nobility was presumed to represent their interests for them. Each estate cast one vote on policy, with the nobility and clergy always being able to outvote two to one the commons, even though by the 1700s the commons represented more people. The demand of the commons to abolish the estate system and replace it with popular representation touched off the French Revolution.

Legal and political equality today are principles in Europe and the United States. In practice, though, far from either has been achieved. It is well known that the poor and the rich have different resources to pursue their interests before the law. Those who can afford more skillful or better-connected lawyers generally fare better. Depending on the voting system in force, the rich and poor also have different resources to pursue their political interests. In the United States, where elections are often decided by the amount of campaign finances that a candidate can raise, those with more money see campaign contributions as shrewd investments.

The eighteenth-century demand for legal and political equality rose against the backdrop of the economic needs of the rising capitalist class. Whether there was a causal relationship, as Frederick Engels held, or merely a convenient one, the effect was the same: formal equality was a necessary condition for further capitalist development.[2] Unequal legal privileges interfered with the efficient production and trade of commodities. If feudal nobles had the power to determine who was allowed to open a particular type of store, then it would be their arbitrary whims rather than market principles that would be determining the nature of commerce. For capitalism to develop, there had to be formal legal and political equality among citizens. Different classes—that is, the nobility and the rising bourgeoisie—could not have different privileges. That was as far as the Enlightenment notion of equality went. It embraced formal legal and political equality but did not challenge the existence of unequal economic and social classes.

If capitalist development required formal—though far from substantive—legal and political equality, at the same time, its economic structure was based on a fundamental inequality between the classes of owners and workers. Any equalization or democratization of the powers between the two classes would undermine the basis on which the system functioned.

EQUALITY OF OPPORTUNITY

Nearly as noncontroversial and universal today as the Enlightenment principles of legal and political equality is the liberal principle of equality of opportunity. The fairest social order, according to this principle, is one in which each person has an equal opportunity to find success in life, most often conceived in terms of economic achievement. Early liberalism seemed to assume that the existence of legal and political equality would be sufficient conditions to produce an overall equality of opportunity to succeed in life. But later, liberalism would realize that those conditions alone would not be sufficient and that further state action would be needed to ensure equality of opportunity, because social position at birth greatly influenced the limits of economic success, even among people who were otherwise equal in terms of their legal and political rights.

By the twentieth century, liberals, especially in the United States, saw public education as the agency par excellence of equality of opportunity. Educational achievement was believed to be the single most important determinant of economic success. Each child in theory equally enters the educational institution, is trained to her or his capacity, and then is able to use that resource to succeed economically.

Much of this optimistic view of what public education could deliver in terms of guaranteeing equality of opportunity was foretold in Emile Durkheim's advocacy of using education to mediate natural and social inequality. He concluded, as mentioned, that public schools would determine different levels of capability among entering students and then train and educate them accordingly—what today is called "tracking," where students are divided into different special-education, vocational, college-bound, and honors streams. The students would come out of the different levels of the educational system prepared to enter different levels of the occupational structure. The different levels of income in the occupational structure would in turn afford different social-class standards of living. If done according to Durkheim's precepts, this stratified meshing of ability, educational training, occupational position, and income would not mimic the distribution of preexisting social classes. Rather, it would abolish hereditary advantages and use individual merit to establish anew each generation the occupants of social classes.

The principle of equality of opportunity thus is fully consistent with and can lead to social inequality. It implies that social inequality will be an inevitable feature and outcome of competitively structured societies. The principle of equality of opportunity reduces to equalizing only the starting points—not the outcomes—of the competitive struggle.

SOCIAL COHESION

A capitalist society can function quite well with equality of opportunity; it could not with equality of outcome. The natural tendency of capitalist development is to polarize incomes between rich and poor. Power to monopolize income opportunities grows with competitive market advantage. Businesses and economic classes rise in the competitive struggle at the expense of their vanquished foes. In time, the victors cumulatively become stronger, and the vanquished slip further behind. McDonald's, the hamburger megacorporation, began with a few stands and then progressively outcompeted family-owned rivals. As it grew stronger and richer, it increasingly monopolized the business and drove family-owned rivals first to lower returns and then completely out of business.

The same asymmetry of power within business classes exists between business and labor. Those who own capital have innumerable advantages over those without it to secure opportunities for higher income. It is business owners, not workers, who set wage scales. Trade unions can attempt to increase wages, but they cannot secure workers higher incomes than their employers.

In a complete laissez-faire capitalism of Darwinian struggle, the rich would eventually monopolize all income opportunities at the expense of all other classes, producing extreme class polarization and inequality. This, though, is contradictory. Extreme laissez-faire capitalism would ultimately self-destruct. Absolute polarization of income would result in economic crisis and breakdown, because the majority of the population would be unable to afford to buy goods and services, causing the collapse of the businesses that depend on their sale. Most likely before reaching that extreme there would be a social breakdown characterized by outbreaks of stealing and other forms of crime by the impoverished majority. The economic and social crises would have the potential of stimulating political crises.

The more laissez-faire or unregulated the capitalism, then, the more it will produce absolute inequality that in turn will provoke economic, social, and political breakdowns of the system. Thus today no one endorses a completely laissez-faire approach to economic and social planning in capitalist societies. But there is a lot of ground between the poles of a savage Darwinian capitalism that produces absolute inequality and one in which counterpolicies are employed to minimize it.

Contemporary conservative, liberal, and socialist ideologists differ in terms of how much inequality they believe can be allowed to exist in the capitalist system without provoking unacceptably high economic, social, or political costs that would be system threatening. That is where social policy comes into the issue, in terms of the degree to which states regulate the amount of inequality that their economies produce.

This is recognized on both sides of the Atlantic. There are differing beliefs, though, over how much the inequality produced by the competitive struggle should be constrained. If both the United States and the European countries share the principle of equality of opportunity, the principle of equality of outcome—that there are social benefits to be gained by individuals and families sharing the same standard of living—is not so shared. The United States has never placed achieving that type of social equality as a goal of social policy. Its Republican and Democratic parties' political platforms have shown no mention of income inequality as a problem to be addressed. The European countries have not made total equality of outcome a goal either, but they have traditionally been more worried about social inequality growing too severe to maintain social cohesion and have adopted counteracting social policies. In 2001, the European Union made an explicit goal of lowering income inequality by 2010 in the interest of advancing social inclusion.

INCOME INEQUALITY

There is no question that income is distributed more unequally in the United States than in Europe. As table 8.1 indicates, according to Luxembourg Income Study information, the distribution of disposable income— income after taxes and including social benefits—in the United States is more unequal than that of all the countries of Western Europe. Income inequality in the United States is 32 percent higher than mean European income inequality. Comparing the earliest years for which the Luxembourg Income Study has information, the 1970s and 1980s, with the latest, 2000 to 2005, income inequality increased in the United States by 17 percent compared to an average 2.6 percent for the Western European countries. During the period covered, while the overall average for inequality increased, it did not increase in all of the European countries. Eight of the sixteen European countries saw modest decreases in their inequality.

INEQUALITY REDUCTION

The state is the only institution strong enough to counter the market's natural tendency to heighten inequality. It can do this directly through the public sector that it controls and indirectly through the taxes that it collects and the social programs that it funds.

Public Sector

The more ownership and regulation the state has, the greater the power it has to diminish inequality. In a completely socialistic economy in which the state owns all means of production and centrally planned economic development, the state could decide as policy how much income inequality there would be and then set wage differentials accordingly. Those wage differentials would then determine the overall inequality in the society.

Table 8.1.   Income Inequality

	Gini Coefficient	Social Distance
Austria	.257	3.15
Belgium	.279	3.30
Denmark	.228	2.78
Finland	.252	3.04
France	.278	3.45
Germany	.275	3.37
Greece	.333	4.73
Ireland	.313	4.48
Italy	.338	4.41
Luxembourg	.268	3.47
Netherlands	.231	2.78
Norway	.256	2.87
Spain	.336	4.69
Sweden	.237	2.82
Switzerland	.268	3.28
United Kingdom	.345	4.46
European Average	*.281*	*3.75*
United States	.372	5.68

Source: Luxembourg Income Study (LIS), "Key Figures Income Inequality Measures Table," www.lisproject .org/keyfigures.htm (accessed March 30, 2010).

Notes: All figures are for disposable income. The Gini coefficient is a statistical measure of overall inequality that ranges from 0 to 1. The closer to 0, the more equal the distribution; the closer to 1, the more unequal. Social distance is the ratio between the incomes of the 90th and 10th percentiles. Data are from 1999 for the Netherlands; 2000 for Austria, Belgium, France, Germany, Ireland, and Spain; 2004 for Denmark, Finland, Italy, Luxembourg, Norway, Switzerland, the United Kingdom, and the United States; and 2005 for Sweden.

That option, though, does not exist for the United States or Europe, where there are mixed economies in which private and public sectors coexist. The presence of the private sector greatly constrains but does not eliminate the ability of the state to control wage differentials. With direct control over only the wage differentials of its own public employees, the state can influence but not completely determine overall levels of inequality, since it has little power to determine private-sector income and wage differentials.

Nevertheless, the greater the proportion of overall employment accounted for by public employment, the greater the influence that state wage differentials have on overall inequality. In both Europe and the United States, public wage differentials are significantly lower than private wage differentials. For that reason, in both Europe and the United States, public employment decreases overall income inequality. Part of the reason, then, why there is less overall income inequality in European countries than in the United States is because they have stronger state sectors of their economies. Public-sector employees constitute on average 16.3 percent of Western European labor forces compared to 14.1 percent of the American labor force.[3]

State policy can influence private wage policy by establishing minimum wages. There is, however, no necessary relationship between minimum wages and income inequality. Minimum-wage increases will only decrease inequality if top incomes do not increase more. Any policy that would attempt to decrease income inequality by raising minimum wages would have to be paired with a means of controlling top incomes.

States can supplement the incomes of poor and otherwise disadvantaged groups. That, though, like minimum-wage legislation, does not necessarily lead to inequality reduction. To the extent that it is based on redistribution of income, it may at the least slow rates of increasing inequality.

State policy can also influence private wage policy indirectly through labor law. The more labor law is structured so as to enable, as opposed to frustrate, union organization, the more unions have the power to increase the relative proportion of public-sector and private company overall compensation that goes to base employees. There are clear differences between Europe and the United States in this respect, as noted. European labor law is much more union friendly, resulting in an average 36 percent of the labor forces of those countries belonging to labor unions compared to just 12 percent in the United States, and 73 percent of European employees being covered by collective-bargaining agreements compared to just 14 percent of American employees (see table 8.2).

In the United States, public-sector workers are much more likely to belong to a union than are private-sector employees. Thirty-seven percent of public employees are union members compared to just 8 percent of private-sector workers, a percentage that is over four times as high.[4] Unionized workers in the United States typically obtain higher pay than their nonunion counterparts. The public-sector and union combination favors lower pay differentials. Private-sector workers have more very low and very highly paid employees than do public-sector workers.

The $400,000 salary of the president of the United States is less than that of middle-level managers of many corporations. It is true that the president is not the highest-paid public employee in the United States. The salary packages of chief executive officers of large public hospitals and very successful sports coaches at public universities can now be in the million-dollar range—still far less than the top-paid private corporation managers, though. But the president's salary carries symbolic importance. Because of their relatively low salaries, many top federal-appointed officials serve for short periods of time and then go on to private-sector positions where they are paid much more, in large part because of the experience and contacts they bring with them from the federal positions.

At the other end of the pay scale, private businesses in the United States are much more likely to have minimum- and sub-minimum-wage

Table 8.2.   Union Density and Collective Bargaining Coverage

	Union Density	Collective Bargaining Coverage
Austria	31.7	98.0
Belgium	52.9	52.9
Denmark	69.1	80.0
Finland	70.3	90.0
France	7.8	98.0
Germany	19.9	61.0
Ireland	31.7	44.0
Italy	33.3	80.0
Luxembourg	41.8	60.0
Netherlands	19.8	79.0
Norway	53.7	70.0
Portugal	18.7	90.0
Spain	14.6	70.0
Sweden	70.8	90.0
Switzerland	19.0	n.a.
United Kingdom	28.0	34.0
European Average	*36.4*	*73.1*
United States	12.4	13.7

Sources: OECD, Trade Union Density in OECD Countries, 1960–2007, www.oecd.org/dataoecd/25/42/ 39891561.xls (accessed March 31, 2010); Lionel Fulton, *Worker Representation in Europe* (Brussels: European Trade Union Institute, 2009); U.S. Bureau of the Census, *Statistical Abstract of the United States 2010* (Washington, DC: U.S. Government Printing Office), table 648.
Notes: Union density is union members as a percent of labor forces; collective bargaining coverage is percent of labor force covered. Data collected 2004–2008.

employees than are public-sector employers. In part this is because private-sector employees are less unionized. In part it is because public employment by its very nature is more open to public scrutiny to avoid underpayment for labor.

There are clear differences between top private managerial salaries in Europe and the United States, with those of the latter being much higher than the former.[5] The differences are artifacts of different corporate cultures within the contexts of different national cultures. Higher managerial salaries for comparable work and responsibilities are considered rational by corporations in the United States because there is little opposition to them within either the corporations or the society as a whole.

The very top incomes in Europe and the United States are based on profits from business ownership. States can regulate to some extent profit income either before the fact, by taxing corporate profits so that there is less of them to distribute to owners, or after the fact by taxing that form of individual income.

Overall, though, the mixed nature of economies in Europe and the United States constrains the power of the state to directly regulate pay and income differentials. Much more effective for increasing substantive equality is to indirectly structure the relative proportions between individualized and socialized consumption.

Socialized Consumption

Corresponding to the proportionate mix between private and public ownership in countries is the mix between how goods and services are distributed through individual and social wages. In the United States, workers receive relatively more of their income than in Europe in the form of individual wages. They use this income to purchase what they need. They pay a lower proportion of their income as taxes but have fewer social benefits than in Europe. Instead, they pay individually for as much as they can afford of health care, child care, education, and other needs.

In Europe, workers receive relatively more of their income as social wages, that is, free access to government-provided goods and services, such as health care, child care, and education, which are consumed in common and equally with other workers. For these higher social benefits, they pay higher taxes.

The reality of the two forms of income is not new. In the first hunting-and-gathering societies, parties went out in search of food that would be brought back and socially consumed by everyone. Today's breadwinners bring back incomes to share with dependents in their households, and welfare states distribute goods and services that are shared by entire populations. The issue for Europe and the United States is the relative proportion of each type of consumption.

It might appear at first glance that the two modes of income distribution have the same overall effect. A citizen can have low taxes and use the savings to purchase health care, or have high taxes and free health care. But there are considerable differences. Privatized services that are individually purchased are inevitably unequal services. The market quickly adapts to the income differences among citizens by offering differently priced access to those services and denying access altogether to those who do not have sufficient purchasing power. If the services are distributed as tax-funded citizen rights, they are more likely to be equally distributed among all.

Thus, the more that income is received in individual wages, the more unequal will be the effect. Citizens will receive different amounts of wages and consequently will be able to afford different amounts of consumer items. The more they receive income in social wages, the more egalitarian will be the effect. Substantial parts of their overall incomes will be expended on goods and services, such as health care and education, that are shared equally with others.

The division between the relative proportions of private and social wages varies within as well as between Europe and the United States. Unionized workers in both locations are more likely to have social wages in the form of benefits as a larger part of their total compensation packages than are nonunionized workers. Among private-sector workers in the United States, those represented by unions have 37.1 percent of their compensation in the form of benefits, while those not represented have 27.4 percent as benefits. Public-sector workers in the United States, who are more unionized than private-sector workers, have modestly more of their pay in benefits as a percentage of total compensation. State and local employees have 34.1 percent of their total compensation in benefits—social wages—whereas private-sector employees have 29.2 percent in benefits.[6]

Those who favor distributing as much as possible of income as individual wages argue that it allows more freedom of individual choice. Workers receive most of their income as personal wages and are required to part with relatively little of it for taxes, despite many Americans erroneously thinking and complaining that they pay high tax rates. They are free to use their personal incomes to purchase whatever is affordable that it pleases them to consume. They can pay high premiums, if they choose, for health insurance plans that cover all possible health risks, or they can gamble a bit and save some money by purchasing a different plan that doesn't have full coverage. The private health-insurance market adapts to their freedom of choice—and different purchasing powers—by offering differently priced heath products, a term much in vogue in the increasing commercialization of health care in the United States.

The public approach allows more egalitarian access to basic goods and services that are consumed in common and social solidarity. Individuals have less personal income and pay higher taxes, but they have fewer expenses for a range of services such as health and child care. They do not worry about—they are free from having to worry about—whether they can afford basic health care coverage, since equal access to it, like access to public education, is taken for granted. Even if they are unemployed or their income drops, they know that, should they become injured or sick, they will be able to receive care without incurring enormous debt.

There are different interpretations of the effects of increasing the social proportion of wages. Karl Marx saw it as marking a progressive step forward toward socialism when societies increased the amount of funds deducted from their gross economic products "intended for common satisfaction of needs, such as schools, health services, etc. From the outset this part grows considerably with present-day society and it grows in proportion as the new society develops."[7] Others see partial socialized consumption more as a reform that helps to preserve the capitalist system by avoiding system-threatening absolute polarization of incomes. Whichever the effect, it provides a policy meeting ground for European conservatives, liberals, and socialists. Like the welfare state, conservatives see in social wages a way to socialize charitable obligations, liberals a way to regulate capitalism to avoid its worst features, and socialists a socialist solution to a capitalist problem that is a step toward socialism itself. In the United States, with no significant socialist presence, only liberals inhabit that ground. American conservatives, unlike European ones, seek to minimize, if not eliminate, egalitarian social wages.

Progressive Taxation

It follows that while equality as a social policy goal can be accomplished either directly by redistributing individual wages or indirectly by increasing the proportion of social wages in national income, the latter is the more effective and easier to accomplish. Both strategies require taking, through taxation, income from upper-income groups and then redistributing it to lower-income groups. The first involves either financing supplemental income for the lower classes or targeted subsidizations of their basic expenses in housing, food purchases, medical expenses, and the like.

The second strategy—the easier and more effective—involves using the revenues derived from taxing excess upper incomes to support the programs (education, health, child care, and so on) that are equally distributed to the population. It is easier and more effective because it permanently removes a form of income from the competitive struggle that produces inequality. The first strategy of redistributing individual incomes represents a temporary shift of income to the needy, the occupants of whose ranks change. Not only is the redistribution temporary, but it also occurs as a politically resented aberration in the context of what is considered to be an otherwise desirable competitive struggle for unequal incomes.

Taxing higher-income groups at higher rates and lower ones at lower rates, by its very nature, diminishes income inequality. The extent of equalization depends on (1) the relative amount of income that is taxed and (2) the degree of progressivity of the tax rates. The more taxation there is, the greater the possibility of diminishing inequality. But if only a relatively small amount of income is subject to taxation, no matter how progressive the tax rates are, the overall effect will be small. How aggressively these measures are employed depends on whether conservatives, liberals, or socialists are in power. It depends also on whether there is a desire to have generous publicly financed social programs.

Inequality Reduction in Europe and the United States

What accounts for inequality reduction, then, are the combined effects of state progressive taxation and redistributive social programs. They result in a significant difference between inequality of money income and disposable income—incomes before and after the effects of taxation and social programs. Depending on how progressive state policy is, the distribution of disposable income will be more egalitarian than the distribution of money income.

What is striking, as revealed by table 8.3, is that the distribution of money income in Europe and the United States is virtually equal with Gini coefficients of .45 and .46, respectively. But when the distributions of disposable income are compared, the differences are dramatic—.29 versus .38. What accounts for the difference is that European tax policies and social benefit policies reduce inequality on average by 36 percent compared to the 17 percent reduction effected by American policies, which is less than half as much.

Income inequality, as the statistical information for Europe and the United States indicates, is an equally inevitable outcome of their competitive private-market economies. What is not equally natural or inevitable is how much of that translates into unequal living conditions. Governments have considerable power to use progressive taxation and social programs to temper the effects of the market on daily living conditions. If the United States is more unequal than Europe, as all the statistical evidence indicates, it is because of different political, not economic, conditions.

Table 8.3.   Income Inequality Reduction: Gini Coefficients, 2005

	Money Income	Disposable Income	Percent Reduction
Austria	.43	.27	37.2
Belgium	.49	.27	44.9
Denmark	.42	.23	45.2
Finland	.39	.27	30.8
France	.48	.28	41.7
Germany	.51	.30	41.2
Greece	n.a.	.32	n.a.
Ireland	.42	.33	21.4
Italy	.56	.35	37.5
Luxembourg	.43	.26	39.5
Netherlands	.42	.27	35.7
Norway	.43	.28	48.8
Portugal	.54	.38	29.6
Spain	.49	.32	34.7
Sweden	.43	.23	46.5
Switzerland	.35	.28	20.0
United Kingdom	.46	.34	26.1
European Average	*.45*	*.29*	*35.6*
United States	.46	.38	17.4

Source: OECD, http://stats.oecd.org/Index.aspx?&QueryId=11353&QueryType=View (accessed April 2, 2010).

9

Poverty

Poverty is a relative term whose meaning is found in reference to what it is not. To be poor is to be not rich, or at least not nonpoor—a double negative that in mathematics results in a positive, in this case the original meaning of poverty. Of course, in life, poverty is taken not as a positive but as a negative condition. A poor person is one who lives below some line that separates him or her from others. If poverty is originally relative, it comes to incorporate an absolute meaning. It indicates a condition of life. One lives in poverty, meaning that one lives at a certain deprived level that presumably can be defined, as in a family of four that has an annual income of less than $22,050 is poor—the way that the United States Census Bureau defines poverty.[1]

MEANINGS AND TYPES OF POVERTY

The two dimensions of poverty, relative and absolute, are not at all necessarily correlated. Not all people who are poor in absolute terms are necessarily poor in relative terms, and vice versa. In global terms today, the first-world/third-world and north/south divisions separate nonpoor from poor countries in absolute terms. The average absolute standard of living of third-world countries is not only significantly lower than those prevailing in first-world countries, but it results in living conditions that are deprived in terms of life chances, especially health conditions.

Any notion of absolute poverty assumes a relative comparison. If third-world countries are judged to be poor, it is in relation to contemporary possibilities, which are known because there are first-world countries living them. On the other hand, today's third-world standards of living surpass in important respects those of first-world countries several centuries ago. No matter, then, how absolute a definition of poverty is, it will always incorporate relativity.

Third-world countries thus have high amounts of absolute poverty by contemporary world standards. They differ, though, according to whether they also have high amounts of relative poverty, meaning that there is a significant proportion of the population that lives on dramatically less income than the average. The typical third-world country has high relative, as well as absolute, poverty, because a small minority consumes most of the country's scarce income. But there are also a few third-world countries that distribute relatively equitably their scarce income. Cuba is an example.

First-world countries, which include those of Western Europe and the United States, have low amounts of absolute poverty by contemporary world standards. As in the case of third-world countries, they differ according to whether they have high or low amounts of relative poverty. The United States is the primary example of the former, those of Western Europe of the latter.

In addition to being measured and conceived of in absolute and relative terms, there is also a subjective dimension to poverty. To be poor in either the absolute or relative sense does not necessarily result in a person's considering herself or himself to be poor. It is also true that people can consider themselves to be poor despite not being poor in either of the other two senses. Thus poverty consciousness is a third variable correlated in varying degrees with the other two, and therefore, to some extent, it operates independently.

MEASURING POVERTY

Measuring poverty depends first upon which dimension—absolute or relative—is being considered, and second upon when the measurement takes place—before or after taxes—and the effects of government transfer programs when they take place. The timing of measurement for poverty has the same consequences as the timing of measurement for income inequality.

The notion of absolute poverty incorporates attempts to define a fixed amount of income that is needed to meet basic needs. It is the form of measurement used to establish the official poverty threshold in the United States. Mollie Orshansky, an economist in the Social Security Administration, originally developed the threshold during the Kennedy administration of the early 1960s. Kennedy had made poverty into an issue, in large part because of the influence of American socialist writer Michael Harrington's *The Other America*, published in 1962. Harrington eloquently drew attention to large pockets of poverty in the United States at a time when many were assuming that most were living a middle-class American dream. If Harrington described the reality of continual poverty, then Orshansky, as an economist working within a major government agency, attempted to find a way to measure exactly how many people actually were poor.

She based poverty thresholds first on the cost of an adequate diet and second on the cost of other household needs.[2] She consulted the 1955 Department of Agriculture Household Food Consumption Survey, which concluded that there were four typical food budgets in order of decreasing cost—liberal, moderate, low-cost, and economical. After some deliberation, she based her calculation on the lowest-cost one, the economical. She assumed that for a household to not be poor in absolute terms, it had to have an income of at least three times the cost of the economical food budget to cover the costs of its food and other necessities. Since the size of the food budget depended upon the number of mouths to be fed, she established different poverty thresholds for different-sized households. She also qualified the thresholds according to the age and gender of the head, resulting in 124 categories of households, each with a different poverty threshold.

In January 1964, six months after the publication of Orshansky's exploratory article and after Kennedy's assassination, the new president, Lyndon Baines Johnson, continued the focus on poverty by announcing that a War on Poverty would be the centerpiece of his domestic policy. To implement the antipoverty program, he established the Office of Economic Opportunity. There was, though, still no official definition of poverty, nor was there an estimation of its size. After much discussion, the Office of Economic Opportunity in May 1965 adopted the Orshansky approach as its working definition. In August 1969, the federal government made it the official definition. The Orshansky approach, with built-in adjustments for inflation and slight modifications, has continued to be used in the United States ever since.

Critics of the Orshansky technique for measuring the poor consider it to seriously underestimate the extent of poverty in the United States. They note that it is too rigid to take into account rising material standards of living. In the more than four decades since it was established, new types of necessities have been added to typical household budgets. No one in 1963 could have foreseen that in the future a personal computer, a relatively expensive item, would be considered a necessity. Critics also note that the economical food budget is too low. The 1955 Household Survey considered it to be an emergency—not normal—budget. The budget assumed also, in Orshansky's words, that "the housewife will be a careful shopper, a skilled cook, and a good manager who will prepare all of the family's meals at home."[3] That may be the case with some households with incomes above the poverty line and thus technically not counted to be poor, but it certainly is not the case with all of them. Orshansky herself considers the poverty thresholds to be outdated.[4]

For all of their limitations, though, the Orshansky guidelines provide reliable measures over time of the waxing and waning of antipoverty results in the United States. The first year for which the thresholds were retroactively applied was 1959, and they showed a poverty rate of 22.4 percent. Over the next fifteen years, as a result of War on Poverty programs, the rate steadily declined to 11.2 in 1974—exactly half of what it had started at. That also turns out to be the lowest the poverty rate has ever been. Since 1974, it has fluctuated between a high of 15.2 in 1983 and a low of 11.3 in 2000.[5]

Two general factors are responsible for the fluctuations: the strength of the economy and the expansion or contraction of antipoverty programs. A strong, growing economy expands employment opportunities at higher wages, which decreases the number of persons whose incomes fall below the poverty thresholds. Political decisions are responsible for expanding or contracting antipoverty programs that lift persons and families above poverty thresholds. There appears to be no consensus among the governing classes that the 11 to 15 percent poverty range is too high or that policies need to be developed to lower it.

The other major approach to poverty measurement is to consider it in terms of relative deprivation. Its existence is indicated not so much by not having enough income to afford the bare essentials of physical survival as by not having enough income to participate in what are taken culturally to be the normal day-to-day activities of the community, such as going to a movie, purchasing holiday presents for others, and eating out occasionally. In order to so participate, one must have an income that is within the normal range.

Most analysts of relative poverty set the bottom of what is considered to be normal variously at 40, 50, or 60 percent of the median national income. Most international comparative measures use 50 percent of the median mark. The Economic Commission of the European Union has set it at the higher end, at 60 percent of the median. Others refer to the high-end measure as the "at risk of poverty" line.

For social policies that embrace social inclusion as a primary goal, the relative conception of poverty is the most appropriate. Whereas the absolute measure focuses on physical survival without regard for integration into the community, the relative measure concentrates on integration into the community while assuming that physical survival goals have already been met—an assumption clearly more appropriate for developed than for developing societies.

For developed societies, relative measures of poverty thus inevitably indicate that larger proportions of the community are poor than do absolute measures. If for absolute measures the focus is on determining the proportion of the population that lives in such abject conditions that its physical survival is threatened, for relative measures the focus is on determining the proportion of persons whose incomes are too low to allow them to be adequately socially integrated for the society as a whole to function well.

There is no question that relative poverty is significantly higher in the United States than in Europe. With 17 percent of households living on less than 50 percent of the median income, the United States tops the list in relative poverty (see table 9.1). Underlying the gravity of relative poverty

Table 9.1. Relative and Absolute Poverty, Percent Below Poverty

		Absolute	
	Relative—50% of Median	a	b
Austria	7		5
Belgium	9		6
Denmark	5		
Finland	7	5	7
France	7	10	
Germany	11	7	8
Greece	13		
Ireland	15		
Italy	11		
Luxembourg	8	0.3	
Netherlands	8	7	7
Norway	7	4	
Portugal	9		
Spain	14		
Sweden	5	6	8
Switzerland	9		
United Kingdom	8	16	12
European Average	*9*	*7*	*8*
United States	17	14	9

Sources: Relative poverty—OECD, *Growing Unequal? Income Distribution and Poverty in OECD Countries* (Paris: OECD, 2008), table 5.A2.1; a—United Nations Development Programme, *Human Development Report 2007/2008* (New York: Palgrave Macmillan, 2008), table 4; b—Timothy Smeeding, "Poor People in Rich Nations: The United States in Comparative Perspective," Luxembourg Income Study Working Papers 419 (October 2005), table 2.

Notes: Relative poverty = percent with income below 50 percent of the median household income in 2005; a = percent of population living below US$11 a day; b = percent population living in poverty using 2000 U.S. official poverty line.

in the United States is the increasing marginalization of the poor into urban ghettoes and isolated households that are socially excluded from mainstream patterns of social interaction. Unlike in Europe where social exclusion is acknowledged to be a serious social problem, in the United States social exclusion is at best ignored and at worst welcomed as a justified punishment for losers in the competitive struggle for a living wage or salary.

From the 1970s and 1980s—the first years for which the Luxembourg Income Study has relative poverty statistics—until 2000, most countries saw increases in relative poverty. The average rate in Europe increased by 13.2 percent compared to a virtually identical 13.3 percent increase in the United States. The difference between the two is that the European Union in 2000 took measures to lower its poverty rate by 2010,[6] while there has been no comparable decision in the United States.

POVERTY REDUCTION

Common to both absolute and relative forms of measurement is the issue of which form of income—money (income before taxes are deducted and social benefits added) or disposable (income after the combined effects of taxes and social benefits)—is used to determine the percentage of people below poverty lines.

The more effective the social policy program for reducing poverty, as with general income inequality reduction, the more the rate of poverty will be less for disposable than for money income. With money income being determined by the unregulated competitive struggle, and disposable income by how its distribution is modified by state social policies, it follows that the direct goal of poverty-reduction programs is to reduce the number of people living below disposable income poverty thresholds. The two variables, then, that determine the extent of poverty reduction are—as in income inequality reduction—the two differences between money income and disposable income: taxes (subtracted from money income) and transfers (added to money income).

Progressive taxation in itself reduces the rate of relative disposable income poverty. If the rich lose relatively more of their money income than the poor due to paying high rates of taxes, that action alone will shift relative disposable income downward and lift some of the money income poor out of poverty. The number lifted out of poverty will depend upon the extent of progressiveness of the tax system.

The number lifted out of poverty will also depend on how much of the resultant extra tax revenues from the nonpoor are used to finance transfers to the poor. The more taxes are used to finance transfers to the money income poor, the more of them will be lifted above the disposable income poverty line. The same holds for absolute poverty reduction.

Using the criterion of 50 percent of median income, money income rates of relative poverty in European countries vary from 17.6 to 33.6 percent, while the disposable income rates vary from 5.3 to 14.8 percent (see table 9.2). This indicates that European government poverty-reduction programs have had considerable, though not complete, success. Denmark and Sweden have the lowest disposable income poverty rates at 5.3, with money income poverty rates of 23.6 and 26.7. The cause of their low relative income poverty rates is their aggressive government poverty-reduction efforts that lifted eight out of ten money income households out of poverty.

Public relative-poverty-reduction programs are dramatically less effective in the United States. Following the same criteria for defining the relative poor as those whose income falls below 50 percent of the median, the United States starts out in terms of money income with a 26.3 percent poverty rate and ends up with a not greatly less 17.1 percent rate in terms of disposable income. The 26.3 percent money income rate is virtually identical to the European average of 26.7, as is the Gini coefficient for income inequality. This indicates that the common market economic structure produces this range of poverty. However, the disposable income rate

Table 9.2. Relative Poverty and Poverty Reduction Rates, 2005

	Money Income	Disposable Income	Percent Reduction
Austria	23.1	6.6	71.4
Belgium	32.7	8.8	73.1
Denmark	23.6	5.3	77.5
Finland	17.6	7.3	58.5
France	30.7	7.1	76.9
Germany	33.6	11.0	97.0
Greece	32.5	12.6	61.2
Ireland	30.9	14.8	52.1
Italy	33.8	11.4	66.3
Luxembourg	29.1	8.1	72.2
Netherlands	24.7	7.7	68.8
Norway	24.0	6.8	71.7
Portugal	29.0	8.9	69.3
Spain	17.6	14.1	19.9
Sweden	26.7	5.3	80.1
Switzerland	18.0	8.7	51.7
United Kingdom	26.3	8.3	68.4
European Average	*26.7*	*9.0*	*66.3*
United States	26.3	17.1	34.9

Source: OECD, http://stats.oecd.org/Index.aspx?QueryId=9909&QueryType=View (accessed April 3, 2010).

of 17.1 is significantly higher than any of the European rates, indicating that the United States does far less in poverty-reduction efforts. Whereas the European average is to save seven out of ten of its money income poor from disposable income poverty, the United States prevents only three out of ten from that fate.

When poverty is considered according to the absolute criteria employed in the United States—the original Orshansky definition and a much lower standard for measurement of poverty—the results of poverty-reduction efforts and other government transfer programs in the United States appear more effective. In 2005, the U.S. government officially defined 12.6 percent of its citizens to be poor in terms of money income before taxes. That figure, though, because of the way the Census Bureau does its calculations, included transfers. If money income alone were considered, the poverty rate would have been 18.9 percent. The net result of government taxes and transfers (including antipoverty programs), using the higher 18.9 percent figure as the starting point, was to reduce the rate in disposable income terms to 10.3. Almost half (45.5 percent) of the money income absolute poor were lifted out of poverty.[7]

U.S. redistribution programs to mitigate poverty seem reasonably successful only when the standard is set very low. However, even when doing that, the results do not look favorable in comparison with those of Europe. Applying the same low standard for establishing money income poverty thresholds to European countries indicates that their much more encompassing and generous transfer and poverty-reduction programs lift much higher percentages of the money income poor out of poverty.

The comparative ineffectiveness of poverty-reduction programs in the United States reflects a lack of consensus in the governing classes regarding making poverty reduction a public policy priority as it is in Europe. High priority, instead, is given to reducing the costs of antipoverty programs. Since the Johnson administration (1963–1969), poverty reduction has virtually vanished as a national issue.

In the 2008 Democratic Party presidential primary, which was ultimately won by Barack Obama, John Edwards briefly broke the silence by prominently focusing on poverty reduction in his unsuccessful campaign. After withdrawing from the race, Edwards joined with antipoverty activists, organizations, and experts to launch a "Half in Ten" campaign. Their goal was to cut the rate of poverty in half within ten years through such policy measures as indexing the minimum wage to the medium income. Because Edwards was considered to be a prominent contender for a cabinet position if Obama won, there was considerable belief that poverty reduction could become a focus of domestic policy for the first time since the 1960s.

Within months of the launch of the Half in Ten campaign, though, and before the November election, revelations emerged that Edwards had fathered a child with a campaign staffer. The ensuing scandal forced him out of consideration for a role in the future Obama administration.

The Obama administration has not made poverty reduction a direct domestic policy priority, no doubt because it considers it to be too controversial in an American political context. It has limited itself to pursuing policies, such as health care reform, that are indirectly beneficial to the poor and the near poor.

THE POLITICS OF POVERTY REDUCTION

There are two polar approaches to antipoverty social policy: a conservative approach that attempts to maximize the private economy and individual choice and responsibility, and liberal and socialist approaches that rely primarily on state-sponsored transfer programs and social solidarity. The set of policies in any given country will usually combine elements from both, though in different proportions.[8]

The conservative agenda on poverty in the United States calls for reliance on the private economy, individual responsibility, and the use of charities and means-tested public programs, when necessary, to deliver relief to the poor. Contemporary American conservatives argue that it is possible for the private economy to grow enough to eliminate absolute poverty at the money income stage. If the private economy grew enough, the poor would receive enough additional money income to afford amounts of food and other necessities that would be sufficient to lift them out of absolute poverty, and this could occur despite their receiving the same or a lesser share of national income. Thus, in the American conservative view, the main thrust of any antipoverty policy should be to concentrate on absolute, not relative, poverty reduction and to promote the growth of the private economy rather than state transfer programs.

Underlying the American conservative view is the belief that people are fundamentally responsible for their fates in the competitive struggle. The best way to end poverty is not through a state-sponsored handout to the poor but rather through reforming the poor of their defects in motivation and educational preparation so as to enable them to compete effectively in the market.

It is no accident, given a growing conservative influence over federal social policy, that the 1996 Welfare Reform Act in the United States, which mandated a cut in direct benefits to the poor, was titled "The Personal Responsibility and Work Opportunity Reconciliation Act." It cleverly

combined for political purposes the positive-sounding values of conservative individualism with the originally Protestant work ethic—both deeply
entrenched values in American culture.

When the problem of poverty undeniably presents itself, American
conservatives call for relying on private charities rather than state-
sponsored efforts to deliver needed resources to the poor. Aside from
avoiding swelling the size of state budgets—a negative to be avoided in
conservative eyes—relying on private charities has the additional advantage of promoting free choice. Only those citizens who wish to do so will
contribute goods and services for poverty relief, and they will be able to
choose the type of poverty relief they wish to support by virtue of the type
of private charitable program to which they give.

Compassionate conservatism, as propounded by the Republican Party
in the United States, reproduces faintly the original Augustinian conservative doctrine of noblesse oblige. In the contemporary market-oriented
version, American conservatives will only interfere with market outcomes of poverty on their own terms of free choice—that is, through
freely chosen charitable contributions rather than through obligatory
taxes for poverty relief. This gives them the power to control directly
what types of handouts they will make.

When private efforts prove insufficient, American conservatives back
limited government relief efforts through means-tested poverty-reduction
programs. These programs differ according to whether their goal is to deliver direct relief to the poor through income supplements, food stamps,
rent subsidies, and the like, or whether their point is to reform the poor so
that they can compete more effectively in the market. Where the latter is
the goal, teachers, job counselors, social workers, and other middle-class
professionals increasingly become direct beneficiaries, since the antipoverty programs finance their livelihoods.

Democratic president Bill Clinton's 1996 welfare reform resulted not so
much in reduced spending on antipoverty programs as it did in shifting
from direct benefits to poor individuals and families to support for reform
programs, including support for the middle-class professionals who staff
those programs. It thereby broadened the class base of beneficiaries of
antipoverty programs. On this, there is a policy meeting ground between
American liberals and conservatives: conservatives ideologically prefer
reforming the poor of their presumed defects, while liberals often staff
the programs.

The fundamental problem with the conservative approach is that it
is not possible for an unregulated market economy to eliminate relative
money income poverty and the social exclusion it causes. That can only
occur on the disposable income level, and only after substantial redistribution. The unavoidable reality is that state action is the only available

means for mitigating the extent to which the competitive market struggle results in the negative social outcomes of relative poverty and social exclusion from the society as a whole.

Poverty reduction inevitably requires transferring resources to the poor. Some of these—as conservatives would have it—can come from private charitable donations. But charity has never proven to be a sufficient source of funding for antipoverty programs. In addition, charitable funds are also rarely distributed equitably or rationally according to needs among the poor. They are distributed according to the desires of the donors.

By far the largest share of poverty-reduction funds must come from public tax revenues. These provide relatively reliable amounts of revenue that can be used to fund poverty-reduction programs, which states have the capacity to design according to rational and equitable principles, even if in reality that does not always occur.

Taxation, then, is at the center of poverty reduction, for it provides the largest potential source of revenues for antipoverty programs. The more tax revenues there are, the more it is possible to fund poverty-reduction transfer programs. Whereas citizens can decide individually whether to donate to charities to help the poor, citizens cannot decide individually whether to pay taxes that are used to help the poor.

All transfer programs involve individual taxpayers contributing more or less than they will receive in resulting benefits. A direct one-to-one relationship between individual input and resulting benefit occurs rarely if ever. To that extent, transfers are almost always involved in government taxation and expenditures. Taxpayers who do not own cars do not receive direct benefits from government road building. A part of their income is transferred to car owners who benefit from the roads.

The concept of transfers, though, is usually meant more narrowly to include only government-financed social programs that involve allocated incomes or supplements to income, such as unemployment compensation, Social Security retirement income, disability payments, and poverty relief. These programs differ according to whether most or all citizens benefit from them at one time or another or whether they are targeted only for the certifiable means-tested poor. Unemployment compensation, Social Security retirement income, disability payments, and family allowances are examples of the first type of generalized transfer programs. Despite not being directly tied to poverty reduction, generalized transfer programs are more responsible for actual poverty reduction than are means-tested programs that are directly tied to it. Expansion of Social Security retirement income in the United States, for example, was more responsible for lowering elderly rates of poverty than were means-tested poverty-reduction income supplements.

A given country can thus obtain more in the way of poverty reduction through the expansion of generalized transfer programs than through direct means-tested antipoverty programs. Conversely, any lessening of generalized transfers will have a significant negative impact on poverty reduction. Generalized transfers carry the additional advantage of enjoying more public political support than do programs that directly target the poor, who are often, at least in the United States, stigmatized and accused of being undeserving of help.

10

Unemployment: The Sword of Damocles

> Unemployment is the sword of Damocles that hangs over the neck of every worker.
>
> —Humberto Silex, labor organizer, El Paso, Texas

Unlike poverty, unemployment is a specifically capitalist problem. It first arose as a problem of economic and social significance in the waning centuries of medieval feudalism as labor markets began to develop and people's livelihoods increasingly depended on securing paid work through those markets.

During the height of medieval feudalism proper, before the development of labor markets, unemployment had not been a problem. Each peasant had a place, however humble, in the estate economies. Nor had unemployment been a problem for earlier Greco-Roman or New World slave societies. It was the nature of the employment that was the problem for the slaves. In the modern era, unemployment was not a problem of any significance for twentieth-century European socialist societies. They were structured to ensure full employment.

Unemployment arose and continues to plague Europe and the United States because of the structural features of capitalism. They create a musical-chairs labor market that at most times has more job seekers than positions. This is unemployment's underlying causal reality, despite many thinking that it is an artifact of personal defects of the unemployed, such as negligence on the job, lack of motivation to work, or lack of sufficient educational preparation. It is undeniable that personal characteristics can determine who becomes unemployed at any particular moment.

But even if every worker had the highest motivation to work and had maximum skills, there would still be unemployment. Engineers, managers, and other highly skilled and presumably motivated workers have all experienced unemployment through no fault of their own.

HISTORICAL ORIGINS

During feudalism's classic period from the ninth to the twelfth centuries, the base of the economic pyramid was made up of peasant labor on manorial estates. Each peasant household had a right to plant crops, graze animals, gather food, and hunt—either individually or in cooperation with other households—for its subsistence needs. In return for these rights, they had rent obligations to landlords, which were paid through work on the landlords' fields.

These were natural rather than money economies. The vast majority of products were consumed directly by their producers. They were not sold for money to others who would do the consuming. There was little money in circulation, with most persons not needing to use it in their daily lives.

There was no labor market. For there to have been a labor market, there would have had to be a group of workers whose labor power was available for purchase by employers. But individual landlords directly tied up peasant labor. In addition, peasants were accustomed to working directly for their subsistence products from the lands, fields, and forests to which they had access. They were not accustomed to working for the more abstract wages that could be used to purchase from others what they needed to subsist. That would only come later with capitalist market economies. Peasants were not accustomed to working for people other than themselves or their landlords. Even if they had wanted to, they were not free to go to work for employers other than their landlords.

If there was no feudal labor market, there could be no unemployment, for unemployment only exists when there are more workers offering to sell their labor power in a labor market than there are employer buyers willing to buy it. This is not to say that there was no feudal poverty or other serious problems. Rather, it is only to say that unemployment, by any modern meaning of that term, could not have existed.

Unemployment in its most basic economic meaning can only exist when labor has become a commodity available for sale in a labor market, and this presupposes that other parts of the economy, including labor products and means of production such as land, have also become commodities. In the full-fledged feudal economy, the basic economic ingredients of labor, labor products, and means of production, of which land was by far the most important, were not commodities. Put differently, there were not markets for any of the three components. No one could buy labor or land, and products could be bought only in scattered, episodic markets.

To make the transition from an economy in which labor, labor products, and means of production were not available for sale to one in which they were took centuries, and it proceeded in fits and starts, with Europe being a patchwork of areas in different stages of development in the transition.

In order for labor markets to develop and for labor to become commodified, peasants had to lose their traditional rights to use the land, fields, and forests of the manors to satisfy their subsistence needs. How this occurred involved considerable social trauma. The earliest and most prototypical case occurred in England. By the last half of the fifteenth century, there had been a general expansion of the production of commodities in England, such that enough of a market economy existed to greatly increase the power of money in daily life. Capitalism thus existed in the circulation of commodities. But it did not yet exist in the production of them. Commodities were not made by wage laborers. They were made by independent peasants and artisans, who were then offering them for sale.

Land was still not commodified in the sense of it being available as private property for purchase. There was a considerable amount of land tied up in state lands, church lands, common lands, and land occupied by peasants. The majority of the rural population was made up of peasants who occupied land that, though it had a feudal origin, was now for all ostensible reasons theirs due to common-law traditions. The peasants tilled their own land and had access to pasturelands to graze their animals and woodlands for wood gathering and hunting. Access to common lands enabled the supplemental production necessary to complete the peasants' subsistence needs. In addition, rarely were there fixed boundaries to whose land was whose. The practice was for one household to till land during one planting season. When the harvest was over, the land would be opened up, along with all other harvested land, to extend pasturage for all of the husbanded animals to use, not just those of the household. For the next planting season, the household might till entirely different land. In time, as capitalism and commodification of land rights progressed, this casual attitude toward ownership and possession would end. Land would be demarcated with hedges and fences for the exclusive use of its owners.

Transformations of labor power and land into commodities went hand in hand in several different ways. Dutch merchants entered England with commodities to sell from the continent and sought raw wool to take back to their own incipient woolen-goods factories. They quickly bought up what was available and then began offering higher prices to encourage English landlords to produce more of it. This gave landlords an incentive to take over and enclose the common pasturelands for their own exclusive use for sheep production. Eventually they demanded exclusive use of all the common lands, denying peasants their traditional rights to them. In time, landlords would take over peasant farmlands as well.

Parallel to the enclosures movement, Henry VIII broke with the Church of Rome and created a division between it and the Church of England. Out of the schism came the English Reformation and the origins of the present-day Anglicans, as they are known in England, or Episcopalians, as they are known in the United States. Prior to the English Reformation, monasteries controlled a considerable amount of land. During and after the Reformation, monastery land was either given or sold at extremely low prices to court favorites, thereby transforming it completely into private property. In the process, many peasants who had been tenants of the monasteries were thrown off. Crown lands similarly, though for different reasons, ended up in the hands of court favorites as private property.

FIRST UNEMPLOYMENT CRISES

As peasants lost access to their traditional lands, which were their means for sustaining themselves, they took to the roads and headed for cities for uncertain futures, in which prospects for survival were problematic at best. The city itself was coterminous with capitalist development. It was in cities that merchants set up permanent sites for markets. It was there that workshops grew into factories. And it was there that labor markets began to develop to find labor for the newly expanding factories. Factory growth, with its demand for labor, would resolve the problem of peasant dispossession of land, but only in the long run.

In the short and medium runs, there were more peasants being forced off the land than there were available jobs in the new factories. The new supply of labor outpaced the demand, with the difference creating a growing unemployment crisis. In classical political economic terms, England for the first time contained surplus labor, not in any Malthusian sense that there was overpopulation, but rather in the sense that there was more labor than capitalistically organized industry could absorb and still remain profitable.

History's first unemployed population had no institutional bases of support to fall back on. They took to the roads, and the roads became dangerous for travelers. They headed for the cities, and the cities became filled with beggars. In desperation, many turned to robbery to survive.

The English Crown responded to the crisis in three ways. First, the Tudor and Stuart kings in the fifteenth and sixteenth centuries weighed in against the enclosures as detrimental to society's welfare. They sponsored a number of ineffectual anti-enclosure measures. These may have slowed down but did not stop the enclosures. In one interpretation, the Crown's posture was nothing more than that, a posture. It responded to the obvious violation of traditional law by proclaiming its allegiance to it but did little or nothing to actually enforce it, because there was a contradiction between the interests of the peasantry, who had traditional right on their side, and the interests of the landlords, who had more access to and class affinity with the Crown. The Crown resolved the contradiction by acknowledging the traditional right of the peasants and officially opposing the enclosures. At the same time, the Crown did little or nothing to actually enforce its anti-enclosures measures, thus allowing them to proceed. A more charitable interpretation holds that the Crown's opposition actually slowed down the pace of the enclosures and thereby gave the society more time to adapt to them, thus sparing it of the most harmful consequences.[1]

A second response was the development of what was the world's first intentional state social policy regarding unemployment. In 1601, Elizabeth I, responding to the poverty and disorder wrought by the enclosures, proclaimed the Poor Law. It assigned responsibility for the poor to local parishes. They were to provide relief for the impoverished old, sick, and infants and to establish workhouses where able-bodied poor were to be put to work. The Poor Law existed in various forms for centuries up until World War II. The distinction between the deserving poor eligible for relief and the able-bodied who should be put to work has continued to be an underlying theme in social policy debates.

The third response, which Karl Marx emphasized in his discussion of the enclosures as one of the forcible measures which created the modern proletariat, was highly repressive.[2] Those dispossessed peasants who were not absorbed in either the factories or workhouses and remained as vagabonds and beggars were subject to the most severe punishments. Marx cited the very same Tudor and Stuart monarchs, including Elizabeth I, who opposed the enclosures, as mandating whipping, branding, slicing off of ears, and death for incorrigible vagabonds and beggars. If direct relief and workhouses were the forward part of the social policy for history's first unemployed, the death penalty was the fallback.

The enclosures and resulting unemployment continued through the seventeenth and eighteenth centuries. These were also the centuries of the beginning of England's colonization of North America and Australia. The colonies became a partial solution to the unemployment problem by providing places to which the unemployed displaced peasants could be exported, thereby relieving pressure on the home country.

While some of the displaced found the means to make the trip voluntarily, most were coerced. It was the practice of the British courts to sentence people convicted of crimes to be exported to the colonies. They then sold the convicted to sea captains who would transport them to North America. There, the captains would sell them to employers as indentured servants. They would be thereby enslaved as indentured servants, usually for a period of seven years. At the time of the American War of Independence, the majority of the white population had arrived originally as indentured servants.[3]

To the English Crown, the policy of exporting the unemployed made perfect sense. It seemed to be a fully humane solution to the problem. The workhouses could absorb some but not all of the unemployed, and certainly exportation was more humane than execution. Underlying the policy was the assumption that unemployment was to be avoided or eliminated at all cost, and that doing so would be economically, socially, and politically beneficial.

That turned out to be a false assumption based on an incomplete understanding of the functioning of capitalism. From the fifteenth to most of the eighteenth century, capitalism in practice was developing in Europe at a faster pace than the understanding of it. It was only in the late eighteenth century that economic theory began to catch up with the reality of capitalist development.

In 1776, Adam Smith published *The Wealth of Nations*, the pioneering work of classical political economy. In it he advanced the famous formulation of what later became known as supply-and-demand theory:

> The market price of every particular commodity is regulated by the proportion between the quantity which is actually brought to market, and the demand of those who are willing to pay the natural price of the commodity.[4]

Smith prominently included labor as one type of commodity, stating that when the supply of it exceeds the demand for it, its price, that is its wage, falls, and vice versa. By implication, an oversupply of labor—unemployment—serves a positive function by regulating the amount of the wage and is therefore not to be viewed in wholly negative terms. Similarly, when there is an undersupply of labor, the wage will rise and cut into the profit of the owner. Rising wages, in turn, attract more laborers into the market, which acts to bring wages back down and shore up profits.

Smith's understanding that unemployment kept wage costs in check and, in more general terms, that it was actually beneficial to capitalist development—or at least to capitalists—spread to factory owners and government officials, and this led them to abandon the policy of attempting to export the unemployed.

ECONOMIC FUNCTIONS OF UNEMPLOYMENT

There are three ways in which unemployment benefits business owners and employers in Europe and the United States. The first, as pointed out by Smith, is that an oversupply of workers lowers the wages that employ-ers must pay and, ceteris paribus, increases their profits. This relationship is immediately apparent to any job seeker. If he or she has a skill shared by relatively few others and there is a demand for it by employers, then wage offers will be relatively high. Contrariwise, if he or she has an ordi-nary skill shared by many or a lack of any particular skill at all and there are many with similarly low qualifications competing for jobs, then wage offers will be relatively low. In the 1990s, for example, as computers were being widely embraced both in businesses and homes, the demand for workers with computer skills was greater than the supply. Computer worker wages rose. But, as predicted by Smith, this enticed many to seek computer training, which increased the supply of trained computer work-ers to the point that it began to match the demand, and wages fell.

Factors of relative supply and demand in the labor market thus func-tion to regulate the wage rate. As demand becomes relatively higher than supply, wages rise; as relative supply approaches relative demand, wages begin to decline. When there is an absolute oversupply, there is unem-ployment, and that serves to depress wages of the employed even more.

It is in the interests of employers to ensure that there is always a ready supply of appropriately skilled workers. Depending upon the field, this can be accomplished by ensuring that public education produces enough graduates with appropriate skills. It can also be accomplished by import-ing workers with appropriate skills.

The second general way in which unemployment is beneficial for em-ployers is that its existence serves to discipline those who still have jobs. When unemployment is high, the dangers of losing a job are high. It is one thing to lose a job when it is relatively easy to find another. It is quite another thing to lose a job when high unemployment makes finding an-other one very difficult. In such conditions, workers are more likely to be especially cautious to preserve their existing jobs. They will be less likely to pressure for higher wages. They will be more likely to work extra hard to win the favor of their supervisors. When unemployment is high, work-ers realize that their jobs are vulnerable too. Layoffs, if and when they come, may be selective. That, then, encourages workers to compete with each other to be on the list that will not be laid off. All of this ultimately results in each employed worker producing more and being more profit-able to the employer.

In the reverse situation, when there is near full employment, em-ployed workers perceive more options if their existing working con-ditions are not to their liking. They can pressure for better working conditions where they are employed, knowing that, should that result in their losing their job, it will not be that difficult to find another. When workers perceive that their employers are having a difficult time finding and keeping workers, they know that they do not have to work as hard to hold on to their jobs.

The effect of unemployment on employed workers operates selectively. It does no good to employed workers for there to be a general low rate of unemployment for the work force as a whole but a high one in their own field. A teacher of physical education, for example, may face a situation in which there are few available positions in physical education regardless of the ups and down of the overall unemployment rate.

The most revealing function of unemployment is that it acts as a shock absorber for the business cycle. Since the beginning of the nineteenth century, when statistics on economic growth began to be kept, it has been documented that market societies go through phases of expansion and contraction. When they are expanding, companies encounter increasing demand for their goods and services. To meet the increased demand, they add employees to their payrolls. When they are contracting, the opposite occurs. The economy slows down, and there are fewer buyers for goods and services. With fewer buyers for what they produce, companies must then reduce production and lay off workers, thereby adding to the ranks of the unemployed.

If companies did not have the flexibility to shed workers as business cycles dipped, they would face bankruptcy. Workers can only be profitably employed so long as the goods or services that they make can be sold. If the product cannot be sold, no matter how productive the worker, the worker must be released. To continue paying wages or salaries to workers to keep producing goods or services for which there are no buyers would result in a drain on company revenues that would ultimately cause financial ruin. Were there to be a law forbidding companies from dismissing even good workers, it would have the effect of severely undermining the ability of companies to survive, let alone prosper, in the ups and downs of the business cycle.

There is thus a functional necessity of unemployment for capitalist economies, though not for all economies. Neither feudalism, as we have seen, nor the Eastern and Central European socialist societies of the twentieth century were structurally dependent on the existence of unemployment. They had problems for sure, but unemployment was not one of them. Whether unemployment is a problem or an advantage of capitalist societies depends on the perspective. It is an advantage from the point of view of employers who wish to keep wages from rising too high, to instill discipline in workers, and to have the flexible means to adapt to the rise and fall of the business cycle. In those respects, it is doubtful that capitalist-organized societies could exist if unemployment was not a possibility. But from the point of view of workers, unemploy-

ment is definitely a problem. It is the sword of Damocles that hang
their necks.

SOCIAL CONSEQUENCES

Loss of income is the first problem when the sword falls. When the pay-
check stops, workers and their dependents lose the ability to continue
making purchases of necessities at the same level. Payment for food, rent,
clothing, and other necessities becomes more problematic. Consumption
of luxuries can be cut back. Strategies can be employed to buy food more
economically. But there is no question that the severity and duration of
lost income undermines the life chances of workers and their dependents.
If unemployment is temporary, household economies will be able to re-
bound with the renewal of income. If it is of longer duration, though, the
household will sink into poverty, and that will bring additional problems.
There is truth in the saying that most Americans are four paychecks away
from poverty.

The unemployed condition is anomic. As originally described by
Durkheim and discussed earlier, anomie is a condition that results from
loss of reference points in life.[5] It can have a number of causes, including
sudden social change, loss of family, and unemployment. Common to
all is disruption of the accustomed, predictable forms of life. Durkheim's
profound insight was that most individuals function best in predictable
routines. They adapt to them. When the reference points that structure
their routines are lost, individuals are left swimming in a sea of stressful
uncertainty.

It is thus not poverty produced by unemployment that is anomic. A
person who has been poor for a long time lives within a relatively predictable situation. It is when poverty comes on suddenly that it is experienced
as anomic, for then the person is thrust into a new, unfamiliar situation.
In the case of poverty produced by unemployment, it would be one thing
if newly unemployed persons were assured that they were being laid off
only for a fixed amount of time and then would be reemployed in their
old positions. Then they could hunker down financially and live off of
savings or income from temporary jobs, knowing that there was indeed
a defined light at the end of the tunnel and that life would resume in its
familiar structures and routines.

But that is not the common unemployment situation. More likely is
that they will not know when or if the unemployment will end. And even
if they are fortunate enough eventually to find new positions, it will not
be known ahead of time what type of positions they will be and at what

ny, the fear of finding a replacement position at a
omic as the fear of not being able to find any at all.
nty that faces the newly unemployed that is experi-
ssful, and hellish.

vious psychological toll that anomic unemployment
results in early death. Among the studies that have
confirmed ... onship between unemployment and early death are
those of Brenner, who found that as unemployment rates increased in the
United States and the United Kingdom, so too did death rates. Stefansson
found the same relationship in Sweden, where the long-term unemployed
had a 37 percent higher death rate than the employed population.[6]

Unemployed persons can die early from a number of causes. In the
United States, where most access to health care depends on medical insurance that is employer provided, loss of employment results in loss of
health care. It is not so much that the unemployed are then completely
unable to be cared for in emergencies. Should an unemployed, uninsured
person be in an automobile accident, for example, she or he will be taken
to and cared for in a hospital, and only later during recovery will they
have to face the hounding of medical bill collectors. Rather, the more
likely scenario that results in early death is that, without medical insurance, people are more likely to avoid or put off being seen medically
in a timely manner for conditions which then become serious and life
threatening. Still more likely as a cause of early death is the very anomic
consequence of unemployment, which results in stress-related conditions
such as heart disease, strokes, and substance abuse.

In addition to early death, which is the most serious possible consequence of unemployment, there can be a host of other negative impacts,
including increases in family tensions and problems.

From the point of view of the society as a whole, unemployment results
in social exclusion, since employment is the most important means of
connecting individuals to the economic structure in a double sense. By
working, individuals contribute to and, more importantly, take part with
others in economic production. This integrates them into a central activity of the society. And, because of the income derived from employment,
they are able to consume goods and services within the normal range of
expectations for the society.

Unemployment breaks these nexuses to social inclusion and integration. To the extent that social inclusion is considered to be a necessity for
healthy social participation, it follows that any condition, such as unemployment, that precludes social inclusion will result in problems. Individuals who are prevented from participating economically in production
and consumption will be prone to becoming detached and isolated from
other social activities. That can lead to depression, loneliness, aberrant be-

havior, becoming withdrawn, and becoming neglected by others. The less people take part in normal social and economic interactions, the higher the potential social psychological toll.

SOCIAL POLICY

Unemployment exists for structural and personal reasons. The dynamics of the capitalist labor market create two types of structural unemployment. In the first, a total type of occupation is made redundant because of productivity increases. The classic example is farming. As agricultural labor becomes more productive due to the incorporation of labor-saving technology, fewer farmers are needed to produce the same quantity of food. Unemployment then grows among the ranks of agricultural labor. The same can be said for the history of mining and for many types of factory employment. The second type of structurally caused unemployment results, as we have seen, from downturns in the business cycle that cause workers to be laid off at least temporarily.

Personal unemployment results from conditions that make individuals unemployable because of their own characteristics, such as health problems, physical or mental limitations, lack of skill, and in some cases motivational problems.

The more laissez-faire the approach to economic and social planning, the less that can be done about either structurally or personally caused unemployment. If profit making is the unchallenged goal of all enterprises, then workers will not be hired if they cannot be profitably employed, and they will be shed whenever their employment ceases to be profitable.

The structural incapability of the private market to generate full employment produces the necessity of a state unemployment policy. The two overall policy alternatives for treating unemployment are maximizing employment or maintaining the population that cannot be employed.

Maximizing Employment

There is a consensus on both sides of the Atlantic that employment is the preferred solution to unemployment whenever possible. The state has three strategies to maximize employment: by stimulating growth policies, both long term and as counters to business-cycle downturns; by subsidizing private employment in unprofitable positions; and by directly creating state positions that are unprofitable.

The first is the least controversial since even laissez-faire advocates see promoting growth policy as a proper role for state activity. Growth promotion can be generalized when state central banks lower credit rates to stimulate borrowing and economic activity. It can be selective when states make investments to stimulate activity in particular regions or to shore up or stimulate particular business sectors or companies. An example of regional stimulation was the policy of the United States government to increase military spending in the South during the 1960s, both to combat southern poverty and to more closely integrate the region into the national union. An example of shoring up the business sector was the federal grant to airlines following their loss of business after the September 11, 2001, World Trade Center attack in New York.

The second and third alternatives are more controversial, since they call for creating unprofitable work opportunities that run against laissez-faire principles.[7] Subsidizing private companies to create unprofitable positions in order to generate employment occurs episodically and is usually targeted to treat particular problems. Examples include paying companies to employ inner-city youth and physically or mentally handicapped persons. Direct creation of state positions—dismissed derisively as make-work by critics—is more controversial from the laissez-faire point of view, since it both allows unprofitability and expands the size of the state sector.

The contradiction between work and profit is well exemplified by the history of President Franklin Delano Roosevelt's Works Progress Administration (WPA) during the Great Depression in the United States. The mandate of the WPA was to create work that made use of the actual skills of the unemployed. Masons were employed to build stone structures. Artists were employed to paint murals. The WPA began with the notion that it was more dignifying to employ the unemployed than to hand out relief to them. As such it embraced the American work ethic and became one of the most popular of the New Deal programs. Despite its public popularity and support, though, it was discontinued in the early 1940s because it had become clear that it cost more to create and administer the positions than to distribute a minimal relief check to unemployed workers. In other words, the business principle of profitability—in the form of reducing costs in this case—triumphed over encouraging the work ethic. Business interests also attacked the WPA because they saw it as providing an alternative form of employment offering choices more desirable than their own low-wage job offers.

If businesses can only accept employment that is profit generating, then workers can only accept employment in a decent job. For workers, the goal is not any type of employment but rather employment with at least an average wage and working conditions that allow socially inclusive normal participation in society. Slavery, it is often said, had full employment. Thus, employment maximization, as policy, has internal contradictory class components.

Unemployment rates in Western Europe until 2008 were an average 3 percent higher than those in the United States (see table 10.1), which would seem to indicate that the latter was more successful at maximizing employment. This, however, is illusory, if the standard of employment at a decent job is used. The United States counts part-time employees as employed. It has relatively more low-wage workers than European countries do. Also relevant is the fact that in the United States the unemployed receive significantly less support than in Europe. This makes them more desperate to accept any type of work to survive.

Unemployment Relief

Public relief for the unemployed differs greatly in the United States and Europe. The United States has a minimalist approach based on the dual premises that unemployment is a temporary condition and that support for the unemployed should not be so generous as to act as a disincentive to those seeking or returning to work. Consequently, the amount of salary replacement during the time of unemployment benefits is low and the duration of the benefits short.

The 1935 Social Security Act established the current system of unemployment insurance. The federal government maintains an unemployment insurance fund based on payroll deductions from workers and tax payments from their employers. This fund is then distributed to the states to finance their own unemployment benefit programs. The amount of the benefit varies from state to state. On average it replaces 49 percent

Table 10.1. Unemployment Rates, 1990–2008

	European Union-15	United States
1990	8.1	5.6
1996	10.1	5.4
1997	9.8	4.9
1998	9.3	4.5
1999	8.6	4.2
2000	7.7	4.0
2001	7.2	4.7
2002	7.6	5.8
2003	8.0	6.0
2004	8.1	5.5
2005	8.1	5.1
2006	7.7	4.6
2007	7.0	4.6
2008	7.1	5.8
Average	*8.2*	*5.0*

Source: OECD, *Employment Outlook 2009*, table A.c.

of lost income during unemployment. Common to all state programs is that benefits will last for twenty-six weeks. Congress may approve up to two thirteen-week extensions if it deems that poor economic conditions warrant them. In the past, the maximum length that anyone could collect unemployment benefits was one year. However, in 2009, because of the severity of the recession, Congress began funding additional extensions beyond one year.

There is no backup system for when unemployment benefits are exhausted, short of welfare programs that require proving indigence. If no employment is found once unemployment benefits end, then workers are without any source of income and must turn to family and friends for help, or they must begin to liquidate savings, including those for retirement and higher education for children. Once those sources are liquidated, people may then qualify for poverty relief. The thrust of welfare cutbacks in the United States since 1995, though, has been to make even poverty relief, like unemployment benefits, temporary. It is now possible to exhaust all forms of public relief.

Western European systems generally have higher income replacement amounts, longer durations of benefits, and backup income replacement systems for when direct unemployment benefits are exhausted (see table 10.2). The exceptions are Ireland, with the same replacement rate and duration of benefits; the United Kingdom, with the same duration of benefits but a higher replacement rate; and Greece, with a lower replacement rate but longer duration of benefits.

What is most notable is that all of the European systems have backup income replacement programs, though less generous, for when unemployment benefits are exhausted. Those systems help to keep the long-term unemployed from sliding into poverty, while in the United States the long-term unemployed must prove poverty before becoming eligible for additional benefits, which in itself are rarely sufficient to lift them out of poverty.

Some of the problems faced by the unemployed in the United States are precluded for their European counterparts because of the relatively greater proportion of social wages. For example, the great majority of working Americans receive health insurance as a benefit of their employment. If they lose their employment, they lose their health insurance. They are of course free to buy a private policy. But heath insurance is very expensive, a cost that is especially out of reach for most of the unemployed precisely because it would come at a time when income has been drastically reduced. Where health insurance comes as either a citizen right, as in Sweden, or an employment benefit that is automatically extended to the unemployed at public expense, as in Germany, the negative impact of unemployment on health is greatly reduced. The 2010 Health Reform in the United States, as discussed in chapter 13, will partially miti-

Table 10.2. Unemployment Benefits: Europe and the United States, 2007–2008

	Percent Income Replaced	*Duration of Benefits in Months*
Austria	52	9
Belgium	58	Unlimited
Denmark	70	48
Finland	65	23
France	71	23
Germany	65	12
Greece	47	12
Ireland	49	15
Italy	63	7
Luxembourg	82	12
Netherlands	n.a.	38
Norway	66	24
Portugal	80	24
Spain	64	24
Sweden	60	14
United Kingdom	53	6
European Average	*64*	*20*
United States	49	6

Source: OECD, Tax-Benefit Models, www.oecd.org/document/3/0,3343,en_2649_34637_39617987_1_1_1_ 1,00.html (accessed April 5, 2010); and OECD, *Benefits and Wages 2007*, table 1.1.

Note: Net replacement rate is an average of cases of a single person and one-earner married couple, an average of cases with no children and with two children, and an average of cases with previous earnings in work at 67 percent of the average production worker (APW) level, 100 percent of APW level, and 150 percent of APW level.

gate but not eliminate the negative impact of the loss of employer-based health insurance.

The danger of unemployment, from the European point of view, is that it leads to social exclusion if countermeasures are not taken. The issue for social policy is how to maintain the unemployed population in a socially inclusive manner. Providing them with income replacement meets part of the problem. With income, the unemployed can continue to at least meet their material needs. But it is not sufficient to avoid completely the dangers of social exclusion. An idled worker is one who by definition is not participating with other working members of society.

Idled workers may succumb to remaining isolated in their homes, slumped in front of televisions. Idleness then has the danger of sending the unemployed into depression and making them unemployable. To counter the social isolation of the unemployed, a number of European countries now offer the unemployed social insertion incentives, such as free access to movie theaters and museums, to get them to leave their homes and participate in public life.

11

Support for Child Raising

Children and old persons, with few exceptions, are dependents. Their ages place them before and after the ages of being economically active and able to support themselves directly. They survive on the basis of support from economically active age groups. Both depend upon the economically active age groups' being willing to extend that support and on the degree to which it is extended.

In the most extreme capitalism, everyone fends for themselves in a Darwinian struggle of all against all. There is no logic within the market that provides for children and the elderly, who cannot directly provide for themselves. There is no inherent market mechanism that ensures there will be transfers of income to support them. For that to occur, nonmarket mechanisms must be in place to offset the market's tendencies to only reward the economically active and successful. The extent to which these mechanisms are in place and their nature depends upon the society's formal and informal family policy.

Family policy itself is a subset of overall social policy, though there is no clear line that distinguishes it from other types of social policies. If family policy is to be made up of all policies that impact the family, then virtually all forms of social policy would have to be considered. The existence or nonexistence of universal health insurance, for example, has great importance for household budgets as well as the health of families.

Today, state-sponsored family policies encompass all programs that attempt to either support or orient how families function. Examples of the former include cash transfers and tax benefits for families with dependent children. Examples of the latter include programs that encourage or discourage child bearing as well as those that promote birth control and family planning. Most analysts consider family policy to be directed mainly at issues regarding children. But in chapter 12 we will consider family policy to be also made up of programs that seek to subsidize or socialize the costs of caring for the elderly, because they, like children, are generally incapable of totally taking care of themselves or of being cared for completely by their families.

THE FAMILY AS CHILD WELFARE PROVIDER: PAST AND PRESENT

Historically, families took direct responsibility for the welfare of their dependent children according to their needs. In the absence of aid from states or other institutions, the family was often the only institution that distributed goods and services according to need rather than productive economic contribution or power.

The farm family of the past functioned as both an economic and social unit. It combined the labors of as many of its members as possible to produce household consumption needs. Children did chores as economically productive contributors.

As societies became industrialized and urbanized, children's labor became less economically important. Children shifted from being productive contributors to the family economy to becoming completely dependent on others who brought home incomes. At the same time, workplace and home became increasingly separated in time and space—a development that Max Weber found to be particularly important.[1] Overall, families became less directly production units and more consumption and reproduction—in the sense of species reproduction—units.

Families were still responsible for bringing up children. But now having children represented more taking on new expenses rather than making investments in the farm's collective labor power, and families became less able to financially support grandparents and other members too old to work. This growing development undercut the financial stability of individual families, prompting the modern social welfare need to socialize some of the expenses of raising children.

SOCIALIZING THE COSTS OF CHILD RAISING

Supplementary state programs to economically support families with dependent children first arose in Europe for a number of reasons. The growing expenses of raising children in urban settings led to falling birth rates.

In the early twentieth century, a number of European countries noted and became concerned about these falling rates. Their response was to develop state-support policies to encourage women to have more children.[2]

Also driving the need for supplemental state support of families with children has been the increasing proportion of two-wage-earner families. As women have moved into paid labor forces, they have had to use earned wage and salary incomes to pay for services such as child care that were formerly done by themselves. The market has proven to be a poor provider of those services at affordable prices, causing the need for state action. As the additional contributions of female workers to family incomes have moved from being supplemental to necessary, any interruption in the provision of these incomes, such as during and after the biologically driven cycle of child bearing, can have serious consequences for household budgets. State or employer programs to make up for incomes that would otherwise be lost become an increasing necessity for these periods.

The basic premise of extending benefits to families with dependent children is that all adults, including those without children, should share to some extent the costs of raising society's children because society as a whole benefits from having children adequately reared. Children grow up to take over the responsibilities of maintaining the survival of the society. They will also be available to provide needed services to both their own parents and aging adults who did not raise their own children. An aging adult who did not have children may need the services of a younger doctor who was raised by someone else.

The counterargument, most associated with conservatives in the United States, is that child raising is the exclusive responsibility of individual families. Not only is there no communal societal responsibility, but it is alleged that the taking on of such responsibilities by society weakens the self-reliance of families.

At the crux of this debate are ideological responses to historical and technological changes that have affected the family. Urbanization and the entrance of actual and potential mothers into paid labor forces are the most important. These have made families increasingly dependent on the outside economy. This has generated the basic issue of the extent to which the costs, risks, and responsibilities of child rearing should be socialized.

The key question for family social policy, as we have seen, is who is responsible for financing the upkeep of children, who themselves are not yet economically productive. There are two possible responsible parties: their families and the state, with individual families having the brunt of the responsibility in most cases. In modern societies, children can no longer be expected to contribute significantly to their own upkeep beyond household chores or part-time jobs as they approach majority age.

For children without families, the state or private charities must step in with support. These include orphaned and abandoned children, children whose parents are in prison, and children whose parents are judged unfit to raise them. State options in these cases include establishing orphanages or attempting to place children with families. In the latter case, the state can pay foster parents to take care of children temporarily or for the long term. It can also promote permanent adoption. In all cases, the key variable is the amount of tax-based contributions that are available for financing.

For children with families—the vast majority—the key issue is how much their costs will be subsidized by taxes drawn from the whole society. Here, two issues are at play. The first is demographic. To the extent that states judge themselves to be underpopulated or the average ages of their populations to be too high, they can encourage couples and women to have more children by providing more support for them. Western and Central European countries that are, because of aging populations, facing long-term imbalances between those who pay into supporting welfare-state programs and those who draw benefits from them have an interest in increasing birth rates. They have all instituted generous child subsidy programs in part because of this motivation. The United States, which is facing the same demographic problem, has not instituted such programs to nearly the same degree, nor is there public discussion of such programs.

The second issue is moral and ideological. To the extent that the principle is embraced that all adults are responsible for all children, programs will be instituted to share the costs of child rearing. This principle, though, while consistent with European social democratic and Christian democratic thought, collides with the principles of individualism and individual family responsibility that are embraced by American conservatives.

The differences between Europe and the United States in this respect are real and significant. But embracement of the individualistic responsibility ethic is not absolute in the United States. As in the case of support for unions and national health care, a majority of Americans may well be favorably disposed to European approaches to supporting families. Having majority backing, though, does not necessarily translate into having the power to institute a program.

Beyond providing access to free primary and secondary education, which is noncontroversial on both sides of the Atlantic, there are a number of programs for subsidizing the costs of raising children. These include family allowances, which are regular cash stipends to families with children; one-time cash, goods, or services grants upon the birth of a child; extra aid for adopted and disabled children; and childcare programs.

There is great variation within Europe and the United States in terms of the types of programs available, whether they are targeted or universal, and how generous their benefits are. As expected, European families receive far more social support for raising children than do families in the United States, though because of the complexity of the programs, it is difficult to quantify exactly how much more.

In what follows, we will concentrate on those family policy programs that are directly targeted toward subsidizing or socializing the costs of child raising in the order to which they affect parents: maternity and paternity leaves, family allowances, child care, and public education. Other programs that benefit both families with and without children, such as universal health insurance, are discussed in later chapters.

Maternity and Paternity Leaves

The arrival of a new child, either through birth or adoption, presents working parents with considerable time and money expenses. For these reasons, private and public plans have been developed in many countries to help parents. These plans vary between allowing unpaid leaves of absence from the workplace to granting paid leaves of absence at varying proportions of salary replacement.

The International Labour Organization (ILO) of the United Nations in 2000 established international standards for maternity-leave programs. These standards include the following: leaves should be for at least fourteen weeks; they should be paid at minimally two-thirds of what the woman was earning; there should be medical insurance; and, in the case of women not eligible for employment-tied benefits, they should receive comparable benefits from general social-assistance funds.

In 2007, all Western European countries, with the exception of Norway, exceeded the standard for weeks of maternity leave, and all except Ireland and the United Kingdom exceeded the standard for wage replacement (table 11.1). Almost all of the European programs are financed through general governmental social-assistance funds.

The United States did not meet either of the minimum ILO standards. Before 1993, it had no national provision for maternity leave. In that year, the U.S. Congress passed the Clinton administration's Family and Medical Leave Act, which allows twelve weeks of unpaid maternity leave, but only for employees who work for companies with fifty or more employees and who meet other working-hour requirements. As a result, coverage is far from universal, with only 60 percent of workers being eligible.[3]

Though there is no national policy guaranteeing paid maternity leaves in the United States, they are partially available as fringe employee benefits in both the public and private sectors. Only a quarter of American

Table 11.1.   Maternity Leaves, 2006/2007

	Weeks	*Percent Wage Replacement Paid*
Austria	16	100
Belgium	15	75.3
Denmark	18	100
Finland	17.5	96.6
France	16	100
Germany	14	100
Greece	17	100
Ireland	48	37.9
Italy	21	76.2
Luxembourg	16	100
Netherlands	16	100
Norway	9	100
Portugal	17	100
Spain	16	100
Sweden	12	80
Switzerland	16	80
United Kingdom	39	23.8
European Average	*19*	*86.5*
United States	12	0

Source: OECD family database, www.oecd.org/dataoecd/45/26/37864482.pdf (accessed April 6, 2010).

employers give fully paid leaves of absence to give birth, with these usually being for fewer weeks than the ILO standard of fourteen.[4] With over half of American mothers with children under one year of age in the labor force, the absence of comprehensive national paid maternity leave continues to be a serious problem, especially for young families.[5]

Many European countries also have parental leaves that allow either parent to stay at home to care for the new child after the exhaustion of maternity-leave benefits. Finland allows twenty-six weeks of parental leave at 70 percent of salary after the exhaustion of maternity benefits at the same rate, with additional parental leave at a flat rate available until the child is three. Such leaves are unavailable in the United States, either as national programs or as job-related fringe benefits.

Family Allowances

Family allowance programs exist in all European countries to subsidize families with children through cash payments. They started in part as a measure to encourage having children in order to offset declining national birthrates. Some of the early programs only gave benefits to families after the birth of a third child. These have been significantly altered so that they all now provide cash benefits after the first child. In Finland, up to 85 percent of the cost of raising a child is subsidized through family allowances. In general, European family allowances are worth about 10 percent of average wages per child. Their impact is greatest for large and low-income families.

The United States has no existing family allowance program. What exist instead are tax deductions for children that are worth about 6 percent of the income of an average family.[6]

Child Care

With the increase of two-income families, child-care programs have become increasingly necessary. All European countries have developed such programs, though with different levels of support. The French program is the most generous. It provides eight hours daily of free child care for two- to six-year-old children. Child-care centers exist for under-two-year-old children in which parents pay income-related fees, with national and local governments subsidizing on average 75 percent of the cost. The United States has yet to develop a national program, relying instead on market-provided programs and some targeted state-subsidized programs and tax breaks.

Public Education

The one universal welfare program that has become available in both Europe and the United States is free public primary and secondary education. It represents a primary example of socializing the costs of raising children to the whole tax-paying society. It occasionally sparks opposition from taxpayers who either do not have children or whose children have grown up. If not on the principle itself of paying taxes for public education, these taxpayers often vote against initiatives to build new schools or otherwise increasing the tax costs of public education. For the most part, though, universal access to and the responsibility for paying for public education are firmly embedded principles.

Universal compulsory education became an issue in the nineteenth century for a number of reasons. As societies industrialized and urbanized, the needs for basic literacy and numeric skills in labor forces became clear. There were other benefits to having educated populations as well. Educated populations could be assumed to be more culturally developed and better equipped to understand, defend, and perpetuate national identities and interests. Educated populations could be assumed to be able to participate better in democratic decision making. Individual families, though, could not be counted on to have the means or will to pay for the education of their children. Industry, individual families, and the state thus found a common interest in socializing the costs of education.

From the perspective of Emile Durkheim, universal compulsory public education gave the state a needed means for rationally selecting and appropriately training future occupants of positions within labor forces characterized by increasingly complex and specialized divisions of labor.[7] It also gave the state an institution to socialize citizens with functional secular values. Public education as a source of generating common values moved into a vacuum created by the declining influence of religion.

Universal compulsory education also became a means of furthering the goal of equality of opportunity. Liberal proponents, including Durkheim, believed that equalization of opportunity was not just an issue of fairness or social justice. It was also a condition necessary for the optimal functioning of the economy. To ensure that the most able persons occupied key positions within the division of labor, there could be no artificial advantages created by social privileges. This led Durkheim to the radical conclusion that inheritance must be abolished—as Marx and Engels had advocated in *The Communist Manifesto*—since it interfered with rational staffing of the division of labor.[8] While that has nowhere occurred, there have been various national attempts to restrict its influence by taxing inherited wealth.[9]

The educational institution should, according to Durkheim's prescription as mentioned, evaluate the abilities of all students regardless of social background and then educate and train them accordingly for future positions in the division of labor. This would create what later would be called a meritocratic society, in which power and privilege would be based, not on inherited wealth, but rather on ability as determined by educational attainment.

Equalization of educational opportunity today, though, is subverted by the widespread practice of the rich sending their children to expensive private schools where they are not subjected to the same meritocratic leveling processes. It is also subverted from within public education by practices that allow for the intergenerational transfer of what Pierre Bourdieu called cultural capital.[10] Children from professional families enter public school systems possessing cultural advantages that are recognized and rewarded as if they were innate abilities. Their home-acquired values and language abilities are more consistent with those rewarded by public school systems than are those of cultural minorities and lower classes.

An additional problem with public education attempting to provide the basis of a meritocratic social order based on educational ability and attainment is that it narrows the range of human abilities to the strictly educational. The ability to raise children—unarguably central to the reproduction of any society—does not figure in an educational attainment–

based meritocracy. As in the general problem that equality of opportunity inevitably produces social inequality, an educational system that focuses only on equality of educational opportunity will be consistent with and contribute to social inequality in the larger society.

To the questions of how much and what types of education are necessary, there are different answers. There is consensus in Europe and the United States that primary and secondary education should be compulsory and free, but there is little consensus over how much postsecondary education should be made available at state subsidy. In general, the pattern was for the European approach to restrict university education to a relative few but make the cost for it free or low, while the American approach was, and continues to be, to encourage the majority of postsecondary students to enter universities but at little-subsidized and high personal cost. In the 1980s, 60 percent of Americans versus 30 percent of Europeans aged twenty to twenty-four attended universities.[11] The most recent figures, though, show a narrowing of the gap, with 65 percent of Americans entering colleges and universities versus 51 percent of Europeans. There are clear differences between European countries. Norway, Finland, and Sweden now have higher participation rates than the United States, while Belgium and Germany remain in the lower 30 percent range.[12]

From the middle nineteenth century, American education reformers rejected a European model of providing vocational education for most while reserving university education for the few. The American dedication to equality of opportunity required that universities become vehicles for that opportunity and thus be open to all comers.[13] At the same time, as Americans have allowed the gap between ordinary and university-trained pay levels to grow, Europeans have traditionally dignified ordinary vocational work so that a socially inclusive normal livelihood could be obtained from it.

The costs and resultant market values of American higher education are unequal. Both private and public systems have greatly higher- and lower-status institutions. In some cases, there are marked differences in what is taught, learned, and carried into the labor market in terms of skills and preparation. In other cases, it is not so much the content of the knowledge taught or fostered that is at issue as it is the social status of the degree. While it is quite possible to obtain a first-rate university education from a low-status institution, this would be at the cost of the educational capital that the status of the degree carries in the labor market.

Behind these different approaches is the question of whether it is necessary for a majority of postsecondary students to attend universities or whether vocational training, or perhaps no additional training, would be sufficient. Despite the almost universal rhetorical belief that the United

States and Western Europe have become knowledge-based societies that require highly trained labor forces, a significant part of the reason why relatively more Americans attend universities is because of the social reality that a university degree carries more future-income advantages in the United States than in Europe. American families, especially middle- and upper-class ones, consider a university degree to be the absolute prerequisite for success in later life. Not all adolescents, though, even from those classes, find university educations to be either desirable or manageable.

The vast majority of Americans, like Europeans, neither inherit nor have enough wealth to leave to their heirs to ensure comfortable lifetime incomes. Their only recourse is to attain desirable income levels through types of employment for which educational credentials are the tickets to entrance. This occurs in a context in which higher educational attainment enables considerable income advantages over those who do not attain it. Americans thus see higher education as an investment they are willing to make for themselves or their children in future income opportunities, even if it means going into substantial debt.

As university costs have risen significantly in the United States—on a par with rising medical costs—students or parents have had to take out more loans. The result has been a type of peonage for students in which they are required to immediately enter the labor force to begin paying back the increasingly onerous debts.

The European approach, with exceptions, limits entrance to higher education by using competitive application processes, while guaranteeing state support for successful applicants. At the same time, it limits the extent to which higher educational attainment results in income advantages.

CHILD POVERTY AND POVERTY REDUCTION

As a result of the much greater public investment in subsidizing the costs of child raising, the average European rate of child relative poverty of 9 percent is far less than half of the American rate of 21 percent (table 11.2). The lowest rates of child poverty are in the Scandinavian countries, which operate on the social democratic welfare model. In these countries, as well as in France, Belgium, and Spain, children are absolutely privileged in that their rates of poverty are lower than those of the general population. In other European countries, where child poverty rates are higher than the general rates, the gaps are significantly lower than that prevailing in the United States.

Table 11.2. Child Relative Poverty Rates, 2005, in Percentages

	Children (0–18)	*Total Population*
Austria	6	7
Belgium	10	9
Denmark	3	5
Finland	4	7
France	8	7
Germany	16	11
Greece	13	13
Ireland	16	15
Italy	16	11
Luxembourg	12	8
Netherlands	12	8
Norway	5	7
Portugal	17	9
Spain	17	14
Sweden	4	5
Switzerland	9	9
United Kingdom	10	8
European Average	*10*	*9*
United States	21	17

Source: OECD, *Growing Unequal? Income Distribution and Poverty in OECD Countries* (Paris: OECD, 2008), tables 5.2 and 5.A2.1.

Note: Poverty line set at 50 percent of medium income.

12

Support for the Aged

The elderly first became the focus of social policy in the late nineteenth and early twentieth centuries as a result of several developments. As life expectancies increased, more persons outlived their capacities to be productive members of labor forces, swelling the numbers of forcibly or voluntarily retired persons. By the end of the nineteenth century, self-employed proportions of labor forces—mainly family farmers—decreased as employed proportions correspondingly increased. Employees were more vulnerable than self-employed persons to being forcibly dismissed as old age diminished their productive capacities.

As families became less self-employed productive units—as in cooperatively maintaining a family farm or other type of business—and more dependent on income derived from paid employment, they became less able to absorb the expenses of caring for old members who no longer were able to contribute an income from paid employment. The growing inability of individual family units to have the financial resources to care for aged members, along with the growing number of aged persons unattached to young families, prompted the need to devise new ways to provide incomes and other forms of financial support for retired persons.

DEVELOPMENT OF RETIREMENT SYSTEMS

In 1883, conservative chancellor Bismarck, as noted earlier, pioneered modern retirement social insurance, in part to counter the rising influence of the socialist labor movement in Germany. By 1935, thirty-four European nations had followed the German lead and had developed some form of social insurance.

In the midst of the Great Depression, the federal government of the United States responded to the growing need for a retirement system with the Social Security Act of 1935. Like the European social insurance plans that preceded it, it socialized the original nineteenth-century principle of family responsibility for the elderly. Instead of each family being responsible for just its own elderly—which was an inadequate basis for supporting the entire aged population—all families would be responsible for all of the elderly. Family values were writ large into the whole society.

Social Security mandates that all active workers and their employers pay taxes into a fund that supports all retired workers. It is a formula that has worked remarkably well since its inception, producing the federal government's most successful and popular domestic program. Social Security is a defined-benefit system in which participants are guaranteed lifetime retirement benefits in accordance with their contributions.

Employers also began offering defined-benefit pension systems as job benefits. As with Social Security, current workers and their employers set aside a part of total employee remuneration and use this to pay out lifetime benefits to retired workers. Employers saw advantages to offering pension plans because it would reduce employee turnover and the accompanying expenses by rewarding loyalty. Employers also initially saw pensions as a low expense since the money put aside to pay out retirement benefits would not have to be paid out for a long time. However, in time, as workers began to retire and draw private pension benefits, many employers found that they had been underfunding their pension plans and sought a way out of their obligation to pay their employees.

The looming crisis in private pension finances prompted large-scale attempts to move toward defined-contribution systems. In those systems, workers would set aside and invest part of their incomes to create personal investment portfolios to finance their retirements. Employers may—but are not required to—contribute to these funds. Retirement incomes are not fixed and guaranteed, as in defined-benefit systems; rather they are dependent on how well the portfolios fare.

Chile, under a right-wing military dictatorship with neoconservative advisors from the University of Chicago, proved to be a laboratory for these changes. In 1981, it transformed its entire national retirement system from one based on defined benefits to one based on defined contributions. The new system required workers to pay 10 percent of their incomes into private investment accounts while absolving employers of responsibility for any contributions.

Ronald Reagan, who came into office that same year, was not in a political position to completely transform Social Security in the same way. But he was able to take partial steps in that direction. The previous Carter administration had established 401(k) and Individual Retirement Accounts (IRAs) by altering the tax code so that contributions could be made into them with pretax dollars. Its intent was to encourage individuals to save for retirement as a supplement to their Social Security and occupational defined-benefit pensions—the so-called three-legged stool of retirement security.

During the Reagan administration, private employers, with the encouragement of neoconservatives, increasingly began to use the 401(k) to eliminate their defined-benefit pension programs, contrary to the original intent.[1] At the same time, the tax savings diminished tax revenues and shrank future financing for federal social programs, thereby accomplishing another neoconservative goal.

In 1985, the Thatcher government in the United Kingdom passed legislation that encouraged workers with tax rebates to move out of state defined-benefit into private defined-contribution retirement programs.

By the 1990s, however, it was becoming clear that these transformations had not benefited most retirees. They had resulted in significantly lower incomes than would have been obtained under traditional defined-benefit plans. The first wave of Chilean retirees under the new system contained many below the $140 monthly-income poverty level. Administration costs by fund managers had absorbed as much as one-third of their contributions.[2] In the United Kingdom, it was found that administration costs for the new defined-contribution plans were also high and that future benefits would be low. By 2004, many workers were moving back into state pension programs. Defined-contribution plans have similarly failed to live up to promised expectations for retirees in the United States.

DEFINED-BENEFIT VERSUS
DEFINED-CONTRIBUTION RETIREMENT SYSTEMS

The reasons for the comparative disadvantages of defined-contribution plans vis-à-vis traditional defined-benefit pensions for most workers can be seen by examining the guiding principles and organizational mechanisms of the two systems.

In defined-benefit plans:

1. Retired workers receive guaranteed benefits—usually set monthly incomes—based on the number of years employed and the final income that they have.

2. The system is financed on a pay-as-you-go basis. Current workers pay into a pool from which benefits are distributed to retired workers. The system is financially solvent so long as an equal or greater amount goes in as contributions than comes out as benefits. Demographic balances between retired and current workers can affect solvency and force adjustments through either lowering benefit amounts, including through delaying ages of retirement, or by increasing required contributions.

3. The systems are based on an intergenerational compact in which current workers are responsible for supporting retired ones with the knowledge that today's supporters will be tomorrow's supported.

4. The system encourages a collective consciousness since workers as a whole pay into and receive benefits from the funds.

5. Money contributed to the system is dedicated to the sole purpose of financing retirement.

6. The participant does not "own" her or his retirement income. Upon death, it ceases or at most can be continued by a spouse. The purpose of the system is only to provide a secure retirement support.

7. Retirement managers may invest retirement funds. The risks of those investments, though, are borne by employers, since the benefit amounts are guaranteed.

8. Defined-benefit plans follow the social insurance principle of spreading the risks of retirement. Lengths of retirement and amounts of income needed to finance them vary because retirees have different longevities. In social insurance retirement plans, the risks are spread, as in medical insurance, by those who do not need the benefit subsidizing those who do. The healthy and sick pay premiums equally despite only the sick drawing benefits. In defined-benefit retirement plans, it is the same principle of those who need the benefit least subsidizing those who need it most, but in this case the unhealthy subsidize the healthy. The unhealthy—as well as victims of accidental deaths—who live short lives pay in more premiums than they draw out as benefits. The opposite is true for the healthy who live long lives.

In defined-contribution systems:

1. Retired workers receive a variable retirement income depending on how well their individual portfolios of stocks and bonds have done.

2. The systems are financed out of individual savings and investments. Instead of current workers pooling contributions to finance the incomes of retired workers, individuals build up individual accumula-

tions that will be used to finance their own individual retirements, without regard for those of the rest.

3. For that reason, defined-contribution systems breed individual rather than collective consciousness.

4. Defined-contribution plan funds are invested widely in the stock and bond markets and thus go into general capital accumulation rather than being dedicated to financing retirement incomes.

5. Former president George W. Bush and others made much of the fact that individuals own their retirement accounts as accumulated wealth that presumably could go into inheritable estates. This, though, eliminates the social insurance principle of spreading the risks of retirement. Instead of the surplus left over when a deceased retiree does not collect as many benefits as paid in going to support longer-living retirees, it is drained out of the retirement system and into estates that benefit younger workers who are not in need of retirement support.

6. The risks of all investments are borne by individual workers.

NATIONAL RETIREMENT SYSTEMS

In both Europe and the United States, there are publicly financed bases of guaranteed income that nearly all retired persons are eligible to receive. These are supplemented by company pensions. They are then topped off by income from individual investments. For those who do not have enough resulting income from public pensions, private pensions, and investment income, there is publicly financed means-tested income (see table 12.1).

More goes into supporting the first form of income at the base of the pyramid in Europe than in the United States, despite the American Social Security system being the single largest source of retirement income for most persons. On average, seventeen European countries expended 8.4 percent of their gross domestic product on public-financed retirement systems compared to 6.4 percent in the United States.[3]

Company pensions are also increasingly more prevalent in Europe because American employers, largely as a result of decreasing labor union strength, are, as noted, increasingly discontinuing them as fringe benefits.

Essentially, neoconservatives in the United States are attempting an inversion so that individual savings and investments will provide the bulk of the pyramid. Each person will be required increasingly to individually finance her or his own retirement. The problem, though, is that savings are an unstable source of retirement income. They are more likely

Table 12.1. Forms of Retirement Income

	Eligibility	*Financing*	*Functions*	*Principles*
Public Pensions	All citizens or those vested in system	General or payroll taxes	Pay-as-you-go/ transfer of income from employed to retired	Social solidarity
Occupational Pensions	Employees of a particular company	Payroll deduction	Pay-as-you-go/ transfer from employed to retired	Partial solidarity
Individual Savings and Investments	Individuals with portfolios	Individual portfolios	Drawdown in retirement of value of portfolio/ purchase of annuities	Individualism
Supplemental Income for Elderly Poor	Means-tested	General or payroll tax	Pay-as-you-go/ transfer of income	Social solidarity

to be sufficient for those who die shortly after retirement than for those who live long lives. Basing retirement on individual savings, as noted, violates the basic social insurance principle of spreading risks. Instead of the surplus of savings left over when a retired worker dies early going to subsidize the incomes of those who live longer, it goes out of retirement entirely and into inheritable estates.

. The most stable retirement system would be (1) based on a pay-as-you-go defined-benefit basis and (2) comprehensive to include all labor force participants. In this approach, employer-based pensions would be phased out as a national pension system became more comprehensive. Individual savings and investments could continue, but without tax subsidization. Lost tax revenues to IRAs and the like would be redirected to supporting the national system.

ELDERLY POVERTY AND POVERTY REDUCTION

One way to judge the effectiveness of a country's retirement systems— *systems* rather than *system* because many retirees receive incomes from more than one source (such as Social Security, pension income, and individual savings)—is to compare the average poverty rates and incomes of the over-sixty-five population with the average poverty rates and income for all ages. If a goal of social policy is social inclusion so that the retired will have roughly average living standards, then the closer those averages of the over-sixty-five people to total national averages, the better. In other words, there should not be a sharp drop-off of living standards at retirement.

Average elderly poverty rates are higher than overall poverty rates in both Europe and the United States, but much less so in the former. In the Netherlands, Luxembourg, Germany, and France, elderly poverty rates are actually lower than overall poverty rates (table 12.2). Elderly median income in Europe is 84 percent of total median income, compared to 56 percent in the United States.[4] Thus, on both sides of the Atlantic, elderly poverty rates are higher and median incomes are lower than national averages. The greater elderly income disadvantage in the United States reflects the country's greater overall income inequality.

Table 12.2. Elderly Poverty Rates, 2005, in Percentages

	Elderly	*Total Population*
Austria	7	7
Belgium	13	9
Denmark	10	5
Finland	13	7
France	4	7
Germany	10	11
Greece	23	13
Ireland	31	15
Italy	13	11
Luxembourg	3	8
Netherlands	2	8
Norway	9	7
Portugal	17	9
Spain	17	14
Sweden	8	5
Switzerland	18	9
United Kingdom	10	8
European Average	*12*	*9*
United States	24	17

Source: OECD, *Growing Unequal? Income Distribution and Poverty in OECD Countries* (Paris: OECD, 2008), tables 5.3 and 5.A2.1.

Note: Poverty line set at 50 percent of median income.

13

Health Care

It is vital for people to be protected from having to choose between financial ruin and loss of health.

—World Health Organization[1]

In a study of preventable deaths—deaths that could have been avoided with timely and effective health care—the United States ranked last among nineteen industrialized, mostly European, nations. As many as 75,000 American lives could be saved each year if the country achieved average health-care delivery standards. That number would increase to 101,000 if the country achieved the standards of the three highest-rated countries—France, Japan, and Australia. An earlier study more conservatively estimated that each year 18,000 people die in the United States due to lack of health insurance coverage.[2]

With 47 million U.S. citizens lacking health insurance coverage—not counting many millions more whose coverage was inadequate in 2010, the year of the United States' major health reform—it was undeniable that the American system was seriously deficient compared to its European counterparts, where all citizens have full coverage. The problem went further. The United States had—and still does have—the world's most expensive health care system (see table 13.1). Americans pay an average annual cost of $7,290 per person for their health care, over twice as high as the average Western European cost of $3,415.

If there is any area of social policy in which Americans are likely to be aware that their system has flaws, it is in health care. Americans generally acknowledge that their high and rising cost of health care is a problem and that they have less confidence in their health system than do Western Europeans. According to a cross-national Gallup poll, only 56 percent of Americans have confidence in their system compared to 72 percent of Western Europeans (table 13.1).

But Americans are less likely to lay the cause on the privatized nature of their health system, assuming that medical care is expensive by its very nature. The majority of health care spending in Europe is publicly financed. In the United States, the majority is privately financed (table 13.1). The major actors in the American health system—insurance companies, pharmaceutical corporations, and physicians—derive the world's highest health-related profits and incomes, largely because they are immune to government regulation and control as they exist in Europe. With the exception of Dutch specialists, American physicians are the world's highest paid. On average, they receive nearly twice as much income as their European counterparts.[3]

Americans acknowledge that the growing number of uninsured persons is a problem. But they are less likely to be aware that their expensive system ranks poorly in quality as well as coverage. Two issues are involved in determining the quality of health care: the quality of a health

Table 13.1.   Health Care System Financing, Cost, and Public Confidence, 2007

	Percent Public Financing	Per Capita Cost	Percent Confident in Health Care System
Austria	76.4	$3,763	84
Belgium	79.5	$3,595	88
Denmark	84.5	$3,512	77
Finland	74.6	$2,840	83
France	79.0	$3,601	83
Germany	76.9	$3,588	54
Greece	60.3	$2,727	45
Ireland	80.7	$3,424	40
Italy	76.5	$2,686	53
Luxembourg	90.9	$4,162	90
Netherlands	62.5	$3,837	77
Norway	84.2	$4,763	68
Portugal	71.5	$2,150	58
Spain	71.8	$2,671	79
Sweden	81.7	$3,323	77
Switzerland	59.3	$4,417	86
United Kingdom	81.7	$2,992	73
European average	_76.0_	_$3,415_	_72_
United States	45.4	$7,290	56

Sources: OECD, _Health Data 2009_ (Paris: OECD, 2009); Ian T. Brown and Christopher Khoury, "In OECD Countries, Universal Healthcare Gets High Marks," Gallup Poll, August 20, 2009.

Table 13.2. Health Care System Quality and Outcomes

	WHO Ranking	Infant Mortality	Life Expectancy
France	1	3.7	80.1
Italy	2	3.7	81.4
Spain	7	3.7	81.0
Austria	9	3.7	80.1
Norway	11	3.1	80.2
Portugal	12	3.4	80.6
Greece	14	3.6	79.5
Luxembourg	16	1.8	79.4
Netherlands	17	4.1	80.2
United Kingdom	18	4.8	79.5
Ireland	19	3.1	79.7
Switzerland	20	3.9	81.9
Belgium	21	4.0	79.8
Sweden	23	2.5	81.0
Germany	25	3.9	80.0
Finland	31	2.7	79.5
Denmark	34	4.0	79.8
European average	—	*3.5*	*80.2*
United States	37	6.7	78.1

Sources: World Health Organization, *The World Health Report 2000* (Geneva: World Health Organization, 2000), annex table 1; OECD, Health Data 2009 (Paris: OECD, 2009).

care system and the average health conditions of a citizenry. In 2000, the World Health Organization (WHO) ranked in order the quality of the health care systems of 191 countries. All seventeen Western European systems ranked higher than the United States (table 13.2).[4]

American health conditions are inferior to those in Europe in terms of infant mortality and longevity, the two most common measures used in international comparisons. Of one thousand babies born live, 6.7 die within their first year of life in the United States, compared to an average of 3.5 in Western Europe. The average American life span of 78.1 years is 2.1 years less than the average Western European life span of 80.2 (table 13.2).

DEVELOPMENT OF NATIONAL HEALTH INSURANCE

Modern health systems began during the last part of the nineteenth century. Before that, there was little professional health coverage for whole populations and no national plans to provide such coverage. Families cared for, and pooled their financial resources to provide for, sick members. Religious and other charities might be available to help the poor. In

Europe and the United States, early labor unions set up sickness funds for members.

German chancellor Bismarck established the prototype of national health insurance in 1883, in large part to counter the public support the socialist labor unions were gaining from the popularity of their sickness funds. Mandatory contributions from employers and employees funded the Bismarckian system. By the 1920s, a number of European countries, including Belgium, Norway, and Britain, had followed the German example and set up similar models. None of the systems, though, were extensive enough to cover their entire national population, nor were their benefits comprehensive enough to cover all situations. In 1930, social health insurance still covered less than half of the working populations of Europe.[5]

The Soviet Union, beginning in 1917, and post–World War II Eastern European communist countries were the first to establish comprehensive health systems that covered entire populations. Those accomplishments stimulated Western European leaders to establish their own comprehensive systems. In the same way that Chancellor Bismarck wanted to counter the influence of socialist labor unions, postwar Western European leaders sought to counter the influence and appeal of communist parties that were significant in a number of major countries, including Italy and France.

In 1946, following recommendations from the 1942 Beveridge Report, Britain passed the National Health Service Act. Sweden passed similar legislation the same year. By establishing centralized, government-owned health systems, the British and Swedish approaches differed from the Bismarckian social insurance approach. Both represented the first noncommunist approaches to universal health care coverage.

The state thus was the major actor in the development of Western European health systems by either mandating establishment of social insurance funds tied to workplaces or by establishing national health services. Social insurance offered mandated coverage to employed workers, national health services to all citizens. In time, the social insurance systems would develop supplementary government-financed plans to extend coverage to unemployed and other sectors of the population ineligible for workplace-related insurance.

Following passage of the 1935 Social Security Act in the United States, several bills were introduced but never passed in Congress to extend Social Security provisions to health care for the entire population. American labor union leaders supported these attempts to establish national health insurance. But by the 1950s, they adapted to the apparent reality that it was unlikely to be accomplished. Instead, health insurance became one of the issues for which they bargained with management. It became one of the advantages of union membership, since unionized workplaces were more likely to have health insurance as a fringe benefit. Health insurance development in the United States thus partially followed the Bismarckian model in that for the most part it was tied to employment as a fringe benefit. But unlike in Europe, the United States government never established or mandated coverage for all workers or the population as a whole, leaving such coverage up to the outcome of private market-driven activities, labor union collective bargaining, or employer largesse.

If the European health systems were established by government actions, the American system evolved out of patchwork private market opportunities around health insecurities and residual government actions that protected particular populations such as veterans, the elderly, and the poor.

COMPARATIVE HEALTH SYSTEMS

There are three health system models in Europe and the United States. These exist on a continuum between the most market driven and the most government controlled. At the two ends of the continuum are privately organized, for-profit health care that exists in the United States and national health systems—sometimes called the Beveridge model—that exist in the Scandinavian countries, the United Kingdom, Italy, Spain, and Portugal. In between, but closer to the government pole, are the social insurance systems that exist in Germany, France, and the Benelux countries.

In the private health care system of the United States, health care is treated as a commodity that is sold to consumers on market principles. The four major health care actors—physicians, insurance companies, hospitals, and providers of medical goods, such as pharmaceutical companies—operate as private businesses. State involvement and regulation is minimized. Individuals purchase health care services as commodities according to how much they can afford. Those who are ineligible for or who cannot afford health insurance go without.

Most Americans who have health insurance have it as a fringe benefit of their employment. Having health benefits tied to employment is seen by American conservatives as a way to encourage work. Instead of being a right, health insurance is a reward reserved for those who work. It is treated as a commodity that is available only to those who perform adequately in the marketplace.

The obvious problem of tying health insurance to the workplace is that it will not cover the unemployed. There is no national requirement in the United States, unlike in Europe, that employers actually include health insurance as a fringe benefit. This has become readily apparent, as a number of employers have begun to cease offering insurance altogether as it has become increasingly more expensive, or they have begun to require workers to pay out of pocket greater portions of the costs. In a number of cases, employers have begun to cease paying the insurance costs of retirees.

Unlike European social insurance models, in which the state mandates that employers and employees contribute to a fund, there is no such state mandate in the United States. Employee health insurance exists only if employers voluntarily offer it to their workers, or workers extract it as a fringe benefit from them. Therein lies the reason why so many working Americans lack health insurance.

In the social insurance model (Germany, France, the Benelux countries), there are a multiplicity of different health funds attached to unions, cooperatives, charities, and private companies. Employees and employers share payments into different such social insurance funds. Social insurance models have obtained universal coverage by virtue of two features. First, they are mandatory. Employers must offer social insurance plans, and employees must enroll in them. Second, for those who are unemployed or otherwise ineligible for workplace-related coverage, governments have compulsory tax-financed backup plans.

National health services—in the Scandinavian countries, the United Kingdom, Italy, Spain, and Portugal—organize health care as a publicly controlled service much like the provision of public education. Individuals pay for health care services through their taxes and are eligible to receive them by virtue of being residents or citizens of the country, thereby ensuring universal coverage. Governments own hospitals and may directly employ physicians on salaries.

None of the countries' health systems, though, are pure representations of any of the models. All have complex combined features. All have state and private funding. Doctors on government salary coexist with doctors in private practice. Private insurance plans exist alongside social insurance. This has led analysts to conclude that while there are pure models of different types of health systems, in practice all countries combine features from the different models.[6]

The United States, which has the most privately organized system, also has government-financed Medicare insurance for the elderly and Medicaid insurance for the poor. All of the European countries with social insurance or national health systems also allow supplemental private insurance to be sold. If the United States uses government-based insurance to partially compensate for the failure of the private market to find it profitable to cover all citizens, then European countries allow private insurance companies to make businesses out of providing coverage for gaps in national coverage. From the point of view of citizens, purchasing supplementary private insurance is a way of topping off their basic plans.

The difference is that whereas the private market on its own cannot cover citizens who lack purchasing power, government plans could become more comprehensive if that became a budgeted priority, depending upon political conditions.

Mixed systems in Europe, in which private insurance is allowed a role, are a compromise between state-administered provision of basic needs and the market. They ensure universal coverage while allowing freedom of choice of coverage according to the different purchasing powers of consumers. Mixed provision systems, though, inevitably compromise egalitarian access, since they allow more choices for basic necessities to those with higher incomes.

Switzerland provides an unusual example of a European country that has achieved universal coverage with mainly private insurance. But for that to be achieved, the Swiss government had to implement regulatory and supplementary actions that violate pure free-market principles. It requires its citizens to purchase health insurance in the same way that states of the United States require their motorists to purchase automobile insurance. Government regulations then require that private insurance plans pool their funds so that risks are shared equally. That avoids companies' selling policies only to healthy citizens. Swiss national or canton governments then provide coverage for citizens who are unable to purchase private insurance.

REFORM POLICY IN EUROPE

Two questions underlie the politics of health policy: what type of primary model—national health service, social insurance, or private—a country will have and what type of secondary features it will adopt as reforms. Reforms in themselves are neither good nor bad. While often presented publicly as purely pragmatic responses to technical problems, reforms usually carry consequences for underlying social policy goals.

In Europe, the primary issue for health care reform is the extent to which privatization and market features will expand within the otherwise state-controlled or state-regulated health care landscape. It is common to argue in the United States that the generous European welfare state is no longer affordable in an era of globalized competition. That argument, though, is difficult to sustain for health care policy when Europe has achieved universal higher-quality coverage at less than half the cost of the American privatized system. Those who would reform in the direction of the American privatized model seek either to reduce state spending or to increase opportunities for private health businesses.

The underlying question is where the line will be between socialized coverage that is available for all citizens and privatized coverage that is available for only those who can afford it. Private insurance companies and their ideological allies would like to expand the latter. However, the inevitable consequences of adopting more features of privatized health care systems in Europe would be increased health inequality.

REFORM POLICY IN THE UNITED STATES

On March 23, 2010, after a year of contentious national debate, President Barack Obama signed into law the Patient Protection and Affordable Care Act, followed the next week by the Health Care and Education Reconciliation Act. Together they represented the most significant reform of health care delivery in the United States in decades. As important as that achievement is, though, it is not sufficient in depth to close the gap between U.S. and European health standards.

With 47 million U.S. citizens—15 percent of the population—without health care coverage in 2010, the immediate necessity was to devise a national plan that would expand coverage to the entire population. It was not just a question of expanding token coverage—insurance that covers only a few health problems or in which there are substantial costs borne out of pocket by consumers. It was a question of developing coverage in which people would be, in the words of the World Health Organization, "protected from having to choose between financial ruin and loss of health."[7]

The Congressional Budget Office estimated that in 2019, as a result of the legislation, health insurance would be extended to 32 million persons who would not have had it without the reform—a significant extension but still 22 million short of the projected number of citizens and residents for that year. The legislation thus marked progress toward but not achievement of universal health care coverage. The country still remains behind European standards in this and other respects. As Spanish health policy expert Vicente Navarro commented upon passage of the bills, "Despite being a positive step, the reform is still very limited. The best of its insurance proposals are light years behind the rights that any Spanish citizen or resident has. It would be an error for Spain to see these reforms as being relevant for our country. They are not. Their application here would represent an enormous step backward for the Spanish population."[8]

With the reform, the United States remains within its traditional private for-profit approach while inching toward more public organization. As coverage expands significantly, so too will the size of the insurance pie that includes both private and public providers. Private insurers will have

Table 13.3. Reconfiguring Health Insurance in the United States, Estimates for 2019

	Without 2010 Reform Number/Percentage		With 2010 Reform Number/Percentage	
Private Insurance				
Employer-based	162	47.4	159	46.5
Individual	30	8.8	25	7.3
Exchanges	—	—	24	7.0
Public Insurance				
Medicare	61	17.8	61	17.8
Medicaid	35	10.2	51	14.9
Uninsured	54	15.8	22	6.4
Total	342	100.0	342	99.9

Sources: Congressional Budget Office, "Summary of Preliminary Analysis of Health and Revenue Provisions of Reconciliation Legislation Combined with H.R. 3590 as Passed by the Senate," letter to Speaker of the House Nancy Pelosi, March 18, 2010, table 2, http://cbo.gov/ftpdocs/113xx/doc11355/hr4872.pdf (accessed March 29, 2010); 2009 Annual Report of the Boards of Trustees of the Federal Hospital Insurance and Federal Supplementary Medical Insurance Trust Funds, table IV.C1, www.cms.hhs.gov/ReportsTrust Funds/downloads/tr2009.pdf (accessed March 29, 2010).

Notes: Numbers in millions. Due to rounding, percentages may not total 100.

a bonanza of new business, though their relative share of the pie will decrease slightly as public programs expand.

According to the Congressional Budget Office estimates, in 2019, when all features of the legislation have gone into effect, the largest proportion of citizens and residents will continue to receive private insurance as an employment benefit, as they did before the reform. Medicare public insurance, which already exists as a right for those over sixty-five, will cover the next largest group. About half of the expansion of coverage to the uninsured will come from liberalization of eligibility requirements for Medicaid, the program that provides public insurance for the poor. The other half will come from the creation of insurance pooling exchanges for small businesses and for individuals without employer-provided insurance or who are ineligible for Medicare or Medicaid.

The exchanges will be lists of approved private providers who offer insurance with the large-group discounts that large employer-based policies have. For the exchanges for individuals, there will be sliding-scale government subsidies for those making up to four times the poverty rate.

As in Switzerland, beginning in 2014, all citizens and residents will be required to carry insurance or face fines. Large employers will also be required to offer insurance or to pay extra fees.

The legislation established three popular reforms: parents can now carry children up to twenty-six years old as dependents on their policies, insurance companies will no longer be able to refuse coverage for those with preexisting conditions, and insurance companies will not be able to impose lifetime caps on coverage.

In sum, while making progress toward the European norm of universal coverage, the reform will still leave 6.4 percent (22 million) of the population without coverage. The reform's cost-containment features will mark progress toward more efficient health care delivery, but the U.S. system will still remain significantly more expensive than those of Europe. Similarly, increased coverage will lessen but will not close the gap between U.S. and European health conditions. Closing all of those gaps will require further reforms to the reform.

14

———

Ethnic and Racial Policy

In Europe, historically developed nationality differences are dominant sources of ethnic identities, in contrast to the United States where biologically conceived race is the most prominent source. In neither, though, is it exclusively the one or the other. Race is now part of ethnic discourse in Europe, and the politics of separate European, Latin American, and Asian nationality identities have been transplanted onto American soil during past and present migrations.

NATIONAL IDENTITY

Nation, state, and country are concepts that refer to different realities. A nation is a people with a common identity. In its purest expression, it has a common culture and language forged through a common historical experience in a common territory. A state is a government over a people or peoples. A country is a boundaried and governed territory that exists alongside other countries and is recognized as such. In the purest, most integrated example, a given country will be made up of a unitary nation with its own state governance. But most examples are less pure. States often govern over territories that contain peoples with different national identities, creating latent tensions if not full tendencies toward separatism.

National identity is fluid. It results from historical developments. The consolidation of national development into a unitary nation-state is always a matter of more or less. Italy is a successful example of a national identity being forged from regional identities. Yugoslavia is an unsuccessful example. Despite a relatively brief period of a Yugoslavian national identity, the underlying Serbian, Croatian, Albanian, Slovenian, and Macedonian identities splintered in the 1990s after the end of the communist period.

The ultimate solution to conflicts between nationalities is to develop an overall common national identity that subsumes the conflicting ones. Both the United States and Europe have gone through violent internal clashes to develop, in the first case, national unity and, in the second, continental cooperation. The United States violently suppressed Indians, took over through a conquering war the Mexican territories on its southwestern borders, and, in its most costly war ever, put down an attempt by the slave-owning South to secede. As a result of these violent actions, it firmly established a unitary nation-state.

Europe in some ways is going through the same process to establish continental unity. Up through the Second World War, European states battled each other in a distant parallel to the United States Civil War. While there are obvious differences between the two histories, the common thread is that of creating common continental territories with internal peace so that largely common economies can develop and prosper. Seen in this way, contemporary Europe and the United States face each other as economically integrated territories but with differing ethnic as well as social conditions.

The United States has fifty internal states, and the European Union has twenty-five member countries. But there are clear differences. Despite the states' rights rhetoric in the United States, there is no question that state sovereignty is completely subsumed under federal national sovereignty. There is no question that nearly the opposite is the case with the European Union, though some would like to see it evolve toward becoming a suprastate.[1] It exists as a federation without a military to enforce decisions. It is a suprastate only as metaphor and as a goal to some.

To be a real state it must have, according to Max Weber's classic definition, a monopoly control over the continent's means of violence.[2] While the North Atlantic Treaty Organization (NATO) exists to coordinate a number, but not all, of the European militaries, albeit under American domination, and there are tentative talks about creating a future common European military, Europe does not have and will not have for the foreseeable future a common military-backed state. It has, rather, tentative institutions built around the European Union in that direction.

The obvious difference in this respect is that the United States began as a single country with a population scattered among internal states. There were differences among the states. But none—with the arguable exception of that between the slave-owning South and the North—amounted to differences between countries. They reflected instead the classic tension between centralization and decentralization of political power within a country. The issue, which has been a continuing theme in American history, was whether the balance of power should lie with the regional states or with the central government, whether governmental power should be exercised more through state and local governments or more through a centralized federal government. Europe, in contrast, was made up of separate countries, each of which had a clear distinguishing national integrity. Whatever integrity states and local entities had in American history, they did not come anywhere near that of constituting separate nation-states.

The issue for Europe is whether it will be able to create a supranational European identity that will subsume the existing national identities, or at the least be able to function as a quasi-unifying identity. At the present historical point, French persons typically identify themselves as French first and European a distant second. The question is whether at some point in the future this order of identity will be reversed as in the United States, where typical citizens identify themselves as American first and, say, New Yorker or Californian second.

The distance that Europe has to go in this direction is indicated by the continuing existence of very strong subnational identities. Catalans typically see themselves as Catalans first, Spaniards second, and Europeans in a distant third place. In Catalonia and other areas of Europe, there is some evidence that subnational identities are growing stronger in the face of the centralizing tendencies of the European Union and globalization.

The 1994 North American Free Trade Agreement (NAFTA) between the United States, Mexico, and Canada raised speculatively the possible future merging of the three countries into an overall North American continental entity in the same way that the European Union raises the possibility of a future overall European entity. As in Europe, the separate national identities would have to dissolve into an overall continental identity. As in Europe, language differences would impede such a development. An additional problem is that while Europeans recognize fellow Europeans as having something in common, however faint, North Americans do not to the same extent.

The citizens of the three North American countries share the common geographically based identity of being North American. Americans, however, have appropriated the label for themselves exclusively. They identify themselves as North Americans, Mexicans as Latin Americans, and Canadians as Canadians. It is rare for U.S. citizens to think of Mexicans as fellow North Americans in the same way that Danish citizens would think of French citizens as fellow Europeans.

INTERNAL MINORITIES

There are two types of internal or indigenous ethnic minorities in Europe. If a nation-state represents one predominant nationality (the Hungarian state as representative of Hungarians, for example), those members of that nationality who live outside of the boundaries (ethnic Hungarians in Romania, for example) will be minorities. There are many such examples and issues in Europe because the formations of state boundaries for various reasons often did not coincide with the boundaries of national communities, resulting in national communities overlapping state boundaries.

Where nation-states have had substantial numbers of their co-nationals residing just over the borders in other countries, there have always been questions of whether at some point those countries would attempt to annex by force the adjoining territories. Quite often in such cases, especially when the co-nationals constitute majorities in the adjoining territories, there are disputed versions of which state has the historical right to the territory, which can become the justification for an invasion that touches off a war to reclaim it. The existence of a majority of ethnic Albanians in the border province of Kosovo in the then Yugoslavia is an example. The war in Kosovo led to a de facto separation of the province from Yugoslavia. Had Albania been strong enough at the time, it undoubtedly would have attempted to annex Kosovo into a greater Albania, an option that some day may occur.

A second type of European minority is made up of internal and overlapping peoples who do not have full self-determination as integrated nation-states. The Basques and Catalans in France and Spain are examples. As in the previous case of national outlanders, such minorities may also seek to separate from the states that govern over them. The Basque separatist movement contains both people who wish to accomplish full self-determination nonviolently through institutionalized means and an armed movement, ETA—the acronym for Euskadi Ta Askatasuna (Basque Homeland and Freedom)—which is attempting to accomplish it through violent means. It classically represents a movement based on an internal regional minority seeking to establish its own separate nation-state.

Language and land are key, but not exclusive, constituents of separatist national identities. Both outlander and internal European minorities often speak languages that are different from those of the dominant populations of the countries to which they belong. Unique languages often, although not always, provide the ability of nationalities to maintain and reproduce cultural distinctiveness and identity. But while a distinguishing language is frequently a key constituent of a separate identity—the Basques have their own language, for example—it is not always a necessary ingredient.

Muslims, Serbs, and Croatians all spoke Serbo-Croatian in Bosnia, yet they fractured into distinctly separate ethno-national communities during the civil wars of the 1990s.

Land is virtually always an essential ingredient, since self-determination leads to separate state formation. There can be no state without a boundaried, landed basis. There can be no free-floating landless state. In this context, the European Roma represent an aberrant example. While there are Roma dialects and languages, there is no historical, traditional, landed center to the identity. For this as well as other reasons, Roma struggles have never been posed in terms of self-determination through the formation of separate states.

The evolution of internal minority differences has been different in U.S. history. Since state lines in the United States are not nation-state lines, the identity differences between state residents—New Yorkers and Pennsylvanians, for example—are not nearly as pronounced as those between European country residents—French and Germans, for example. Cultural differences exist between the different states and regions of the United States, but they are clearly subsumed within the overall national identity.

The first type of European minority—nationals who live across the border from their home nation-state—do not exist in the United States. One might be from Louisiana and be living in Mississippi, but that is as far as it goes. There is no community of Louisianans living together in a particular border area of Mississippi and preserving a separate cultural identity that would be strong enough to raise the possibility of one day Louisiana attempting to annex that territory, much less going to war with Mississippi over it.

It is the second type of ethnic difference—based upon internal groups that are not linked to other nation-states—that is key in the United States. Indigenous peoples, the original Mexican communities in the Southwest, and black Americans are the most prominent examples. Because these groups have been racially different from the majority white population, contemporary minority issues in the United States have been cast almost exclusively as racial issues, whereas in Europe, where internal minorities—with the exception of the Roma—are racially the same, the issues are cast as ethno-national and cultural.

Racism and *antiracism* as terms are widely used in European policy debates, but they are used differently than in the United States. For the most part, Europeans conflate racial and ethnic discrimination. Ruth Wodek and Maria Sedlak, researchers at the University of Vienna, for example, define racism as "a historically developed system of ethnic or racial dominance resulting in social, economic, political and cultural inequality."[3]

European lack of focus on racial identity is indicated by the lack of official statistics on racial groups. It is impossible to determine from official statistical sources how many black persons reside in Western Europe. Americans, on the other hand, clearly distinguish race from ethnicity. They see blacks as being discriminated against primarily because they are racially, not ethnically, different from the majority. And American official statistics pay careful attention to determining the sizes and distributions of racial groups.

IMMIGRANT MINORITIES

Migration is a relatively new issue for European countries. In the nineteenth century, they were mainly sending countries, with the majority of their emigrants going to the United States in search of better economic opportunities, and in some cases political freedom. Up through the 1970s there was relatively little immigration.

Immigration, though, has always been a central defining feature of the United States. Its national character and identity starts with European immigrants entering its shores in search of better lives. These immigrants quickly outnumbered the sparse indigenous population. Wave upon wave of new immigrants significantly drove the nation's population growth.

The United States, like Canada and Australia, is a classic immigration country. If European population growth has been, until recently, driven by the two demographic variables of birth and death rates, U.S. population growth has been always significantly affected by the third demographic variable of immigration.

Recently, though, immigration has become a more significant issue in Europe. Beginning in the late 1980s, immigration rates jumped in the original fifteen member countries of the European Union.[4] The end of communism resulted in significant emigration from those countries to Western Europe, both because exit controls were eliminated and because privatization and market reforms created significant new unemployment problems. Net emigration from thirteen Central and Eastern European communist countries was 32,800 between 1980 and 1984. Between 1985 and 1989, it jumped to 106,600, a 325 percent increase, reflecting the beginning collapse of communism in those countries in 1989. From 1990 to 1994, it made an even more spectacular jump to 318,400, a 971 percent increase over the 1980 to 1984 period.[5] Immigration in Western Europe further increased because the European Union countries allowed nationals from any member country to work in any of the other countries.

The type of European minority composed of immigrants from other European countries only existed faintly as a parallel in U.S. history. The so-called Okie migration to California during the Great Depression produced an identifiable minority within the latter state. Black and white immigrants from Southern states to the industrial factories of the North often ended up living in the same neighborhoods. Whatever existed of those separate identities quickly diminished though.

Western Europe and the United States today have similar proportions of noncitizen residents—6.6 percent in the United States and 7.6 percent in Western Europe.[6] This overall similarity, though, is deceptive. The vast majority of noncitizens in Western Europe are from other European countries, while the majority in the United States are from developing countries. Thus, while Western European countries have nearly as much multinational diversity as the United States owing to immigration of outsiders, they do not have nearly as much racial diversity due to that migration's being from within the same larger European white population.

Migration from Developing Countries

Both the United States and Europe have experienced strong increases since the 1990s in migration from the developing countries of Latin America, Asia, and Africa. These have obeyed three demographic push-and-pull factors since the end of the Cold War. On the push side, there have been more military conflicts because there is less regional control with only one superpower, the United States. Because of this, there are more refugees fleeing violence.

Second, and more significantly, with the collapse of the socialist countries, the capitalist powers and international institutions such as the World Bank, the International Monetary Fund, and the World Trade Organization have had the unchecked and increasingly unresisted power to transform many economic structures in developing countries to conform them to free-market, laissez-faire patterns. This, usually referred to as globalization beginning in the 1990s, results in destroying forms of production that are less efficient in terms of world market competitiveness but which employ, for sure at poverty levels, many persons. These persons have seen themselves as obligated to emigrate from their homes to search for new sources of income.

At the same time, on the pull side, both Europe and the United States have had increasing need for the labor power of immigrant workers. Immigrant workers fill vacant spots in domestic factories, fields, hospitals, restaurants, and other work sites. Young immigrant workers also contribute needed taxes to support the social programs on which the aging domestic populations of Europe and the United States depend.

International inequality is simultaneously a push-and-pull factor. Over the past decades, while there is evidence that living conditions in most developing countries have improved somewhat as measured by infant mortality and longevity rates, at the same time the gap between these living conditions and those of Europe and the United States has grown.

On the push side, emigrants leave poor countries because they perceive their living conditions to be intolerable. They are pulled to Europe or the United States because living conditions there are perceived to be, and in fact are, more materially favorable.

The domination of international media by the media of rich countries, who are always eager to sell their cultural products as export items internationally, plays a significant role in enhancing this perception. As television has become widespread in the developing world, more people have seen images of better living conditions in Europe and the United States on a daily basis. Such images of dramatically better living conditions, it is not surprising, serve to reinforce inclinations to emigrate. The antiglobalization slogan, "A better world is possible," finds its parallel in the motivation of the immigrant who believes that better living conditions are possible.

The colonial pasts, and in some cases present, play roles in determining the direction of migration flow. There are often advantages for emigrants to move to the countries of their former or present colonial dominators. There may be special laws in place that give them favorable entry. The emigrant is more likely to know the language of the country of destination. Hence France became the destination for Algerians and other members of the former French empire; Britain the destination of Indians, Pakistanis, Jamaicans, and other members of the former British empire; and the continental United States the destination of Puerto Ricans and Filipinos.

Immigrant Death

Many die attempting to reach the United States or Europe. Currently, three hundred to four hundred illegal immigrants, mainly from Latin America, die yearly attempting to cross the stretches of desert along the U.S. southern border. Another one hundred to two hundred drown attempting to enter the United States from the Caribbean areas. Haitians, Dominicans, and Cubans, in that order, mount makeshift crafts and set sail for either Florida or across the strait of Mona for Puerto Rico, from which it is easier to then travel to the mainland United States.

Hundreds of other illegal immigrants, mainly from African countries, drown trying to enter Europe when their makeshift boats capsize in the Mediterranean Sea or Atlantic Ocean. Sub-Saharan Africans attempt to reach Spain's Canary Islands off the northwest African coasts of Morocco and Western Sahara as a way station for getting into Europe, similar to the use of Puerto Rico as a way station for Dominicans attempting to reach the United States.

Agricultural Modernization and Migration: Mexico and Spain

The North American Free Trade Agreement represents the clearest and most instructive example of economic rationalization provoking increased migration from a developing to a developed country. NAFTA required that Mexico progressively remove tariffs on imported foods and other commodities. It allowed American corporate farms to export their huge surpluses at low prices into the country and thereby take away the traditional markets of several million subsistence farmers.

While many of these farmers have been able to hold on to their lands, their grown children have found themselves forced to leave to find adequately paying work. As a result, the 1990s saw a sharp increase in illegal Mexican migration to the United States.[7] Between 1996 and 2001, the size of the unauthorized Mexican population residing in the United States nearly doubled, from approximately 2.35 million to 4.51 million persons.[8]

The NAFTA period has also seen a sharp rise in criminality. Neoliberal laissez-faire reforms associated with NAFTA greatly cut back Mexico's Canasta Básica, or Basic Basket, policy of subsidizing food distribution to the poor. The undercutting of social programs resulted in shattering the fragile degree of social peace that existed in the country. There were sharp increases in illegal drug production and trafficking. According to one estimate, 30 percent of Mexico's cultivated land is controlled by drug cartels.[9] Violence associated with the drug trade has exploded, particularly in the border areas with the United States. The violence is fueled by guns brought in from the United States with its lax gun control laws.

There has also been a sharp increase in kidnappings.[10] These have affected all classes since even ordinary people are targets with ransoms adjusted to their means. The rich remain in mortal fear of kidnappings. Those substantial parts of the Mexican upper classes that supported and gained from NAFTA neglected to consider that without a reliable, uncorrupted police force, the social disorder that resulted from the breakdown in social peace would enter their own houses.

In an editorial, the Mexico City daily newspaper *La Jornada* summarized the relationship between neoliberal reforms and the explosion of criminality. The reforms since the 1980s had shrunk the public sector by privatizing public holdings, loosened regulations on large corporations, weakened *ejidos* (a form of peasant communal land ownership), privatized the social security system, reduced salaries, and treated independent unions with official hostility. The results were catastrophic: growth in unemployment, the informal sector, poverty, and inequality; loss of economic sovereignty to foreign capital; increased migration; and social and family decomposition. Social decomposition, combined with effective weakening of state control, created the space for the explosion of criminality.[11]

It is instructive to compare Mexico's experience of agricultural modernization and rationalization with that of Spain. Both countries began with relatively high proportions of their labor forces in agriculture. In 1990, 23.5 percent of the Mexican labor force was in agriculture; in 1970, 22.8 percent of the Spanish labor force was in agriculture.[12] Both countries witnessed sharp decreases in agricultural employment, with resulting increases in unemployment and migration away from the land. In the case of Mexico, a significant percentage of the emigrants went to the United States. In the 1970s, a significant percentage of displaced Spanish agricultural workers went to Germany and other European countries. In both countries, social programs were inadequate to provide alternative forms of support for the displaced populations. But by the end of the 1970s, a difference would emerge that would make Spain's experience distinct from that of Mexico.

After the 1975 death of fascist dictator Francisco Franco, Spain began a transition to constructing a European welfare state. The socialist governments of the 1980s and early 1990s recovered lost ground from the Franco period in building up the welfare state. Despite eight years of conservative governments from the middle 1990s to 2004, the new welfare state was sufficient to provide enough alternative income and support to displaced workers that migration from Spain has all but ceased, despite the country's continuing to have an unemployment rate of over 10 percent.

Thus Spain, following the Western European lead, built up its welfare state as agricultural workers were being displaced. But Mexico, following the American lead, did the opposite and began to dismantle what few public welfare institutions existed in the country. Spain's direction of reform—toward strengthening social programs—partially compensated for economic displacement and slowed the rate of emigration; Mexico's NAFTA-influenced direction—toward weakening social programs—aggravated the negative social consequences of economic displacement and added to the forces stimulating emigration.

The Spanish example demonstrates that displacement of workers from the land during periods of agricultural modernization need not lead to migration out of the country if the country has strong enough social programs to counteract the short- and medium-run losses of income for those workers. Where such programs are either absent or severely debilitated by neoliberal reforms, as in the Mexican case, out-migration from the land will lead to significant out-migration from the country.

In this respect, multilateral organizations such as the International Monetary Fund, World Bank, and World Trade Organization have stimulated international migration by pressuring developing countries to both modernize their agricultural sectors with free-market reforms and, at the same time, cut back public expenditure on social programs.

SOCIAL POLICY

Max Weber noted that centralization and decentralization was one of the great pendulum movements of historical development.[13] Ancient Rome was highly centralized, medieval Europe highly decentralized. Countries have often fought civil wars over whether to place the preponderance of power and authority in central governments or to federate it to regional governments.

The options of centralization and decentralization exist also in ethno-national policies. The opposing directions are creating a centralized integrated national identity or maintaining pluralistic, decentralized, separate ethno-identities—in current terms, whether to pursue a policy of integration or one of multiculturalism. If federalism is the decentralization of state authority, multiculturalism is the decentralization of national identity.

Assimilation versus Multiculturalism

In the 1920s and 1930s, during the formative period of American sociology, the Chicago school sought to analyze how immigrant minorities became integrated. Chicago was an immigrant city par excellence. Because it was a growing production center and railroad transportation hub, employers were in continual need of immigrant labor. From Eastern and Central Europe came Poles and Czechs. From the American South came whites and blacks. They arrived and fragmented into ghettoized neighborhoods that often spoke different languages. For the Chicago school of Robert Park, Ernest Burgess, and others, the question was how this multiplicity of nationalities would become integrated as Americans.

Out of the Chicago school came the concept of assimilation. The original immigrant generation would be distinctly different from the dominant American nationality. Often it spoke a different language, it had different cultural habits and values, and it identified itself as different. But each succeeding generation's offspring would progressively lose what was culturally different and adopt more of the characteristics of the majority group. In time the offspring of immigrants and native groups would be indistinguishable.

The metaphor of the "melting pot" was meant to capture this process. Some argued that it was a case of the minority completely shedding its original distinguishing identity and adopting that of the native majority. Others argued that the minority and majority cultural characteristics would blend together to produce a new identity that was neither the one nor the other. In all cases, minority members would have to shed significant portions of their original culturally distinguishing identities in order to become integrated and accepted as Americans.

To a large extent, assimilation has been the experience of European immigrants to the United States. Mary Erdmans studied third-generation Polish Americans in the 1990s and found that while they continued Polish traditions in cooking and how they celebrated holidays and practiced their Catholicism, they saw themselves as Americans first.[14]

The assimilationist model, though, came under subsequent critique, especially in the 1960s, and gradually lost ground to a multicultural model. Among the grounds of criticism was the reality that not all minority groups were assimilated. In particular, the mainstream society did not accept and integrate nonwhite minorities as it did European white minorities. The Polish American women studied by Mary Erdmans saw themselves as whites who were different from blacks or from people from Latin America. Racial identity as whites had more importance for them than their ethnic identity as Polish Americans.[15] There was also the question of whether it was necessarily desirable to have all minorities shed their cultural roots as the price of admission to a homogenized American identity.

The multicultural model distinguishes institutional integration and acculturation. Institutional integration refers to minorities' being able to equally participate in economic and political institutions of the society. Acculturation refers to adopting the cultural characteristics of the majority nationality. Multiculturalists maintain that it is possible and desirable to promote institutional integration without requiring full acculturation of minorities. Not requiring full acculturation allows minorities to maintain important cultural roots and identities that enable their families and communities to function better socially. Second-generation children are better able to linguistically and culturally communicate with grandparents. There is more of a smooth transition into learning and functioning in the mainstream culture if parts of the original culture are maintained as backups and defense networks when conflicts with the dominant institutions and culture develop.

Integrating Minorities

Integration is a multidimensional phenomenon with socioeconomic, legal-political, and cultural dimensions.[16] It is also a two-way street in which the dominant society must remove barriers that block the integration of minorities, and minorities must adapt to the practices and acquire the skills that will enable them to be integrated.

Socioeconomic integration refers to whether minorities, either national or immigrant, are able to participate on equal terms with the dominant population in the labor market and the community in general. It is not sufficient for labor force integration to have minorities relegated to the least paid and desirable positions. While it is common to have minorities play economically functional roles as cheap labor, this does not allow their social integration into the community, since their low pay does not afford them the means to participate normally.

Political integration involves acquisition of rights to participate democratically. Immigrant workers contribute economically and most often pay taxes, but most often they are not allowed to vote. This dilemma presents two policy possibilities. The first and more orthodox option is to promote acquisition of naturalized citizenship for authorized immigrants. This in turn provides an opportunity to promote further political and other forms of integration by requiring immigrants to develop sufficient language skills and knowledge of the common principles and cultural values of the society. The second option, underway in some European countries, allows immigrants to vote in local and European-wide, but not national elections. American policy is restricted to the first option. Neither option, though, addresses the political integration of the growing numbers of unauthorized immigrants in Europe and the United States.

Language is the key but not exclusive component of cultural integration. To the extent that there is a dominant majority-minority relationship, facility in the dominant language becomes a survival skill for minorities in the labor market, and a necessity if there is to be any type of unified national culture to undergird national integration. Linguistic integration requires that states develop language-acquisition programs for immigrant and internal language minorities. An important question for policy is the extent to which the state encourages and facilitates maintenance of minority languages as well.

American Affirmative Action and European Positive Action

Affirmative action in the United States and positive action in Europe are the most well-known and controversial policy measures for redressing discrimination against minorities. The premise of both is that when nondiscrimination legislation proves to be insufficient to improve living conditions of minorities, more aggressive measures become necessary.

The term *affirmative action* was first used in the United States on September 24, 1965. President Lyndon Baines Johnson, in response to pressure from that decade's civil rights movement, issued Executive Order 11246, which required nondiscrimination in employment by the federal government and by government contractors and subcontractors. Its section on contractors stated,

> The contractor will take affirmative action to ensure that applicants are employed, and that employees are treated during employment, without regard to their race, color, religion, sex or national origin.[17]

Though the civil rights movement directed itself at discrimination against blacks, the executive order included language to apply its protective provisions to all racial and ethnic minorities, religious minorities, and women. In 1973, disabled persons were added.

The original language directed affirmative action toward ending discrimination in employment. In time, affirmative action would be interpreted to mean ending underutilization of minorities in employment as well. The first meaning is protective but passive. It obliges employers not to discriminate. The second meaning obliges employers to increase the number of minority employees. Between the two meanings lie a host of issues and controversies.

Nondiscrimination laws and policies in themselves are not controversial in the United States. The notion of equal opportunity is deeply ingrained in the national culture. So-called soft affirmative action programs in which employers make special efforts to notify minority members that they are welcome to apply for openings are also not controversial. Public controversies begin with hard affirmative action policies that establish preferences for minorities in employment in order to reach quotas to end underutilization of the minorities. Critics interpret hard affirmative action policies as amounting to reverse discrimination. The controversy parallels Americans' acceptance of equality of opportunity but not result. Americans accept nondiscrimination employment opportunity, but many do not accept policies to ensure the result of actual equality in employment.

Affirmative action policies that give preference to minorities in entrance to universities remain controversial, too. Ironically, white students who resent affirmative action for racial minorities rarely complain about university policies that give preference to athletes. They accept affirmative action to ensure winning teams but not to obtain social goals. Preferences given to less qualified children of wealthy alumni of elite universities have similarly come under little criticism.

Further controversies remain over who the beneficiaries of affirmative action should be. Affirmative action arose in the United States as a policy to achieve equality of opportunity for domestic racial minorities who had been the victims of discrimination, primarily arising out of the history of slavery and conquest. It remains controversial whether affirmative action benefits should apply to recent nonwhite immigrants.

There are still further controversies regarding the factor of class in affirmative action programs. If the goal is to achieve equality of opportunity, then affirmative action should only benefit those racial minority members who are disadvantaged, not middle- and upper-class minority members. If, on the other hand, the goal is to produce racially diverse workplaces at all levels, then middle- and upper-class racial minorities would be eligible.

European positive action policies have the same controversy fault line as in the United States: the public does not resist them so long as they are restricted to ensuring nondiscrimination and preparing minorities to be able to equally compete for jobs. Controversy and resistance begin when the policies mandate that minorities be given preference in hiring.

There are other contextual differences that lessen the similarity of reaction. European positive action programs are not primarily targeted at racial minorities because racial differences as such are not as prominent and divisive there as they are in the United States. There is nothing comparable to the close correlation of class and race that existed with slavery in the United States, and there is no legacy of that institutionalization that presents a continuing problem to be dealt with today. Ethnic, not racial, minorities have been the root internal issues.

On the other hand, a number of European societies, including the United Kingdom, Germany, France, Portugal, Spain, Denmark, Italy, and the Netherlands, held colonial possessions in the past that contained racially different peoples. To the extent that they derived riches from those possessions, they exploited the racially different populations of their colonial empires. The correlation of class and race thus existed in European history, but, unlike in the United States, the racial components were separated in physical space, since the racially different populations lived in distant colonies.

Race, though, is becoming a more significant domestic issue in Europe as increasing migration from Africa, Asia, and Latin America brings in racially different residents, including those from former colonial possessions who often have preferential immigration eligibility. Something similar to the color coding of the American class structure will likely become more apparent in Europe, but not as strongly. What will mitigate against its forming so acutely will be the more developed welfare state, social policy, and greater acceptance of egalitarianism.

To the extent that a relatively greater share of national income in Europe continues to be distributed through social wages rather than individual wages—that is, through access to commonly shared social programs in retirement, health care, child care, and the like—the effects of racial discrimination on standards of living will be lessened. A strong welfare state, while not eliminating the possibility of racial and other forms of discrimination, prevents substantial types of consumption necessities from being affected by discrimination.

Strong welfare programs have the effect of circumventing the cultural and institutional legacies of racial and ethnic discrimination and prejudice to at least partially accomplish the goal of equalization of living conditions. That, of course, by no means lessens the necessity of maintaining and developing policies that combat active forms of discrimination.

15

Incarceration as
Social Policy

In 1986, an assassin gunned down Swedish prime minister Olaf Palme as he and his wife were walking home from a movie in Stockholm. In reacting to the news, Americans were confounded that a prime minister of a country could walk the streets without bodyguards and without fear. They could not imagine an American president and his wife walking alone to a movie theater in Washington, where a president does not step outside of the White House without elaborate and expensive security precautions. Such are the differences between what Americans and Europeans take for granted about the relative dangers of walking their streets.

A culture of violence and fear is firmly interwoven into the fabric of American society. It is more acute in some areas and contexts than others. Some citizens live on inner-city streets where taking precautions against street violence is an assumed part of their daily routines. Others live in relative suburban and exurban safety and circulate through their daily public tasks without fear, but vicariously observe the violence of drive-by shootings in inner cities via nightly television news reports. Distance from street-violence danger has, like income, become an attribute of social class position.

Homicide rate differences are the most dramatic example of the different level of crime in the United States compared to Europe. The American homicide rate is over four times as high (table 15.1). Driving the American rate are widespread gun ownership, a culture of violence, and exclusionary social policy.

If you put a gun on the wall in the first act, wrote Anton Chekhov, you must use it by the third act. In life as in theater, the gun is both

Table 15.1.   Homicide, Gun Ownership, and Incarceration Rates

	Homicide*	Gun Ownership**	Incarceration*
Austria	0.73	30	95
Belgium	n.a.	34	93
Denmark	0.53	12	63
Finland	2.13	45	64
France	n.a.	31	96
Germany	0.88	30	89
Greece	0.98	23	109
Ireland	1.59	9	76
Italy	1.06	12	92
Luxembourg	n.a.	41	155
Netherlands	0.97	4	100
Norway	0.71	31	69
Portugal	2.15	9	104
Spain	0.77	10	160
Sweden	1.27	32	74
Switzerland	0.80	46	76
United Kingdom			
England and Wales	1.41	6	153
Scotland	2.13	6	152
Northern Ireland	1.33	22	88
European Average	*1.22*	*23*	*100*
United States	5.62	89	756

Sources: United Nations Office on Drugs and Crime, Tenth Crime Trends Survey, 2005–2006, table 2.3; Graduate Institute of International and Development Studies, *Small Arms Survey, 2007* (Cambridge: Cambridge University Press, 2007), chapter 2, appendix 5; Roy Walmsley, *World Prison Population List*, 8th ed., International Centre for Prison Studies (London: King's College, 2008).

Notes: * per 100,000 population, ** per 100 population.

metaphor and reality. Part of the reason why there are more American than European homicides is because the instruments to commit them are more prevalent. There are eighty-nine guns per one hundred persons in the United States, almost one per person. It is the highest rate in the world, nearly four times as high as the European average of twenty-three. There are guns in 35 percent of American households.[1] Most civilian European firearms are long guns (rifles and shotguns), which are used mainly for hunting. There are, compared to the United States, relatively few handguns, which are used mainly for personal security and crime.

The pervasiveness of American gun ownership manifests cultural values. The Second Amendment to the Constitution guarantees citizens the "right to bear arms." For many, this is the most important right in the Constitution, a right that in their eyes gives them the ultimate means of protection from tyrannical government. It is suspicion of the state bordering on paranoia that feeds on the values of self-reliance, independence, and freedom. Instead of finding protection in the unity of the community as represented by the state, there is self-reliant protection based on individual ownership of means of violence.

The American desire to own a gun is a predictable response to an American culture of violence. American history has seen an unending series of expansionary wars, from conquest of Indians to obtain land to conquest of Middle Eastern countries to obtain oil. American television has a morbid fascination with violence. In a laissez-faire climate in which anything goes that produces money, American television producers know that they can increase viewership—which increases the rates that can be charged for advertising—through portrayals of violence, since so many people are drawn to it. The oldest tricks in theater to draw attention are to portray acts of violence or sex. In the case of television, either portrayal will cause channel-surfing viewers to stop. The more it is portrayed, the more viewers will stop, in a competition to appeal to ever-shorter attention spans. The more who stop, the more will be exposed to the accompanying commercial message.

For sure, Europe experienced and participated in severe violence during the wars of the twentieth century; and there is no reason to believe that European wartime conduct was any less violent than American conduct. The difference is in peacetime conditions. European domestic relations are far less violence prone than are American ones. To a large extent, the effects of European social policies, in part geared to ensure relative social peace in the sociological sense, result in also maintaining domestic peace in the literal sense.

Americans know they live in a violent reality.[2] They take some small comfort in knowing that a percentage of the perpetrators of illegal violence will face the ultimate form of violent punishment, death. While capital punishment has been abolished in all Western European countries, it continues to be legal in federal law and in most state laws in the United States. The starkly different views of capital punishment in Europe and the United States reflect different cultural and social realities.

So, too, do dramatically different rates of incarceration. As the United States has cut back public antipoverty programs, it has increased spending on prisons and now has the highest incarceration rate in the world at 756 per 100,000 population, almost eight times as high as the European rate of 100 (table 15.1). Even when controlling for the influence of race, American incarceration rates are dramatically higher than those of Europe. There are 487 white Americans in prison per 100,000 members of the population, nearly five times as high as the average European rate of 100. Meanwhile, the rate for American blacks is a staggering 3,161, over six times the white American rate and thirty-one times the European rate.

The rate for Latin American inhabitants of the United States is 1,200, more than double the white rate.[3]

In the eyes of many, a place in prison is increasingly being substituted for a place on poverty relief. At the same time, as public support for the poor has been reduced, there has not been a corresponding rise in living-wage jobs. As the poor are pushed off of welfare rolls, they are lucky to find work. If they do, it is most likely at wages that are not much better, if at all, than the incomes they were formerly receiving on welfare. They make a transition from welfare recipients to low-wage labor, as outsourcing and deindustrialization remove living-wage factory jobs.

In this climate of economic and social desperation, an informal, illegal drug market has grown. It provides physical relief, however palliative, and economic opportunities, however dangerous. Joining the military and risking life in foreign wars provides another draconian alternative to poverty relief.

16

Summary: Principles for Progressive Social Policy

As the previous chapters have abundantly demonstrated, contemporary advanced capitalism looks different in the United States and Europe. In the former, a fundamentalist faith in nineteenth-century laissez-faire economics enjoys considerable influence and power, one of the consequences of which is to minimize state responsibility for social programs. In the latter, the notion that a comprehensive welfare state is necessary to temper capitalism's worst tendencies and features is widely accepted.

For sure, the divide between the United States and Europe in terms of social policy, social programs, and attitudes toward the desirability of having a welfare state is not absolute. There are Americans who would like to see their country move closer to a European model, and vice versa.

When thinking of reforming social policy, therefore, the first question is, reforming it in what direction? *Reform*, as a word, rhetorically appears as a universal positive, like *freedom* and *democracy*. No one in principle is opposed to it, just as no one is opposed to freedom or democracy.

The question is not whether to reform social policy. All programs are in need of constant maintenance, improvement, and often creative changes. The question rather is the direction in which changes are to be made. Should Europeans institute reforms to make their social policy come closer to the American model, or should Americans be seeking to come closer to the European one?

The American model incorporates the values of individual freedom without worrying greatly about community welfare. The European model pays more attention to the social cohesion of the community. Which is the better? The answer lies in the realm of value choices. While social science cannot scientifically determine which values are superior, it can demonstrate that if programs predicated on one or the other are adopted, they will have distinctly different consequences.

The minimalist American welfare state, as we have seen, results in the United States having significantly higher rates of poverty, crime, and other social problems. It follows that if Americans wish to seriously tackle reducing those social problems, and if Europeans wish to avoid increasing their social problems to an American level, then the welfare state and its constitutive social programs in the first case needs to be strengthened, and the second at least maintained.

Critics of the welfare state will counter that there is no longer a choice, because it is increasingly unaffordable. One variation of the argument is that while a comprehensive welfare state was once affordable, it no longer is, largely owing to the pressures of globalized competition. A country must be lean and fit, meaning not having expensive state social programs, if it is to compete effectively. The problem with this argument is that contemporary developed societies are more prosperous now than in the past when they presumably were more able to afford generous welfare programs. If they are more prosperous now than in the past, they are more—not less—able to afford such programs.

The nonaffordability argument substitutes an implied value choice for a supposedly immutable economic principle. All economies produce and distribute. How they produce and distribute varies. With the same amount of production, a society can either distribute it primarily through individual wages and minimal social programs or through lower individual wages and stronger social programs. Resource-wise, both are possible and affordable. In social terms, though, each choice carries dramatically different consequences.

VALUES AND GOALS

Europe and the United States share the modern values that individuals should have freedom and be self-reliant. These are values that were not prominent in early societies, in which individual identities and aspirations were more subsumed within group and community contexts. The members of medieval society largely thought and presented themselves alike in terms of dress, with little or no premium placed on standing out as different from others. The opposite prevails within the modern societies of North America and Europe, in which freedom to think for oneself regarding religious, political, and other beliefs, as well as how to present oneself publicly in terms of dress, is highly valued.

As in the case of integration and multiculturalism forming complementary parts of an approach to ethnic-social policy, the issue is how to combine individual freedom and community welfare into a unitary social policy.

The American approach embraces more individual freedom than community welfare. It holds the corollary values of individual autonomy and self-reliance. The European approach places more emphasis on the shared values of community welfare and social solidarity. Many Americans pride themselves in not being a bother to others, whereas Europeans are more likely to see reaching out to others as cementing their community relations with them.

It would be tempting to make the easy conclusion that the truth lies somewhere in between the American and the European approaches. Averaging, however, is seldom a road to truth. Rather, it is more a question of positing the dialectic of individual and collective identity and welfare in world historical terms.

Individuals in the earliest societies were parts of unitary egalitarian collectivities. The first class divisions within any societies developed around 8000 BC. Those divisions undermined exclusive collective identities, as identities based on more partial and eventually individual interests began to emerge and develop. These new identities, though, never completely displaced or abolished collective identities. Up through the immediately premodern and precapitalist periods, collective identities greatly constrained individual freedoms, which could only fully emerge, as argued classically by Durkheim, with the development of more complex divisions of labor, in which mutual interdependence replaced thought conformity as the basis of social order.

The problem with laissez-faire capitalism, which Durkheim and other liberal theorists recognized and which Marx and other socialist theorists especially criticized, was that it took individualistic freedom too far, to the point that it undermined the social cohesion of societies. The next step forward therefore required resuscitating and expanding on the values of community, social cohesion, and inclusion while at the same time subsuming and reproducing the progressive values of self-reliance and freedom.

The problem with the conservative American approach is that it wishes to move back to exclusive self-reliance and freedom and is therefore reactionary. If Americans need to recognize and put at the forefront the values of community, social cohesion, and social inclusion, Europeans need to maintain and strengthen their commitment to those values and necessities.

The problem with capitalist development is that it will, according to its own logic, move in the direction of values that are consistent with the narrow logic of the market mentality, in which each person competes to maximize individual gain. For social policy to achieve social cohesion and inclusion, it must be willing to temper that internal economic logic, and the only institution that is strong enough to counter that logic is the state. Successful progressive social policy must therefore be lodged in state action.

PRINCIPLES FOR PROGRESSIVE SOCIAL POLICY

Stated formally, there are nine interconnected and overlapping principles that make up a progressive approach to social policy.

Community Welfare

Progressive social policy seeks to maximize the healthy functioning of the community. While concerned with individual welfare, it does not start or rest there. Its primary goal is to produce, as much as possible, a harmonious, healthy integration of the community. It assumes that individuals require both freedom and community support.

Social Inclusion

For there to be harmonious, healthy integration of the community, there must be social inclusion. All members must have sufficient resources to participate in a normal manner in the community. This includes economic resources to maintain a normal standard of living and political resources to participate in democratic decision making. Social programs need to be developed or strengthened to ensure that all citizens—not just the economically successful—have sufficient resources to participate in a normal manner.

Social Solidarity

A guiding ethic of progressive social policy is that each member of the community feel a bond with and be willing to support other members in need. Progressive social policy institutionalizes that ethic through tax-supported social programs rather than leaving it up to voluntary donations to charity programs.

Anomie Prevention

Contemporary rapid rates of economic and social change destabilize living conditions for many. They produce stressful, anomic conditions of life, including sudden increases in unemployment and poverty. They disorient and disrupt accustomed living routines and life progress and thereby undermine social stability.

Progressive social policy seeks through careful planning to guide economic and technological change in order to minimize harmful anomic consequences. Social planning may include the establishment of social programs to aid those affected by needed changes so that they can maintain stable living conditions.

Social Equality and Poverty Reduction

Social equality and poverty reduction are interrelated goals since they enhance a socially inclusive, stable, and integrated community. By social equality is meant not merely equality of opportunity, but also substantial equalization of vital, necessary living conditions, such as access to health care, food, and education.

Since the status of being poor prevents persons from participating in the community in a normal manner by marginalizing them due to lack of economic resources, poverty reduction must be a primary goal of a socially inclusive policy. In that context, poverty, poverty lines, and poverty reduction are more usefully measured in relative rather than absolute terms.

Decommodification

Distribution of vital goods and services, such as health care, food, education, and housing, according to need rather than as commodities according to unequal purchasing power, is a mark of progress in human development. The more that societies have the capacity and the consciousness to decommodify the distribution of vital goods and services, the more they can improve individual and social welfare.

Decommodification requires an economic base of adequate productivity. The more productivity there is, the more economic surplus there is to distribute to maintain at average levels populations that cannot be economically productive, such as children, the disabled, and retired persons. At the same time, shifts in consciousness, including instilling an ethic of social solidarity, are needed so that economically productive and successful individuals will not seek privileged consumption access as rewards and rights. Also needed is a shift of commodity consciousness away from wasteful consumerism to allow production of more necessary goods and services.

Increasing Social Wages

A benchmark of decommodification is the extent to which social wages increasingly displace individual wages. The more national income is distributed as social wages—that is, as socialized and equalized benefits—the greater the progress toward social equality.

Progressive Taxation

Progressive taxation by its very nature is a vehicle for redistribution of income in the direction of equalization. It allows states to transfer income from the privileged via tax-supported social programs to less privileged classes. Progressive taxation does not only benefit the less privileged. It also benefits the privileged, since it increases the effective demand of the lower income groups, which allows the circulation of commodities to proceed. It also benefits the privileged by undergirding social cohesion and peace.

The Democratic State as Agency

The logical agency to strengthen the social bonds of the community is the public authority or state, because it is comprised of the institutions that belong to the people or community as a whole. Partial interests motivate all other agencies—including private businesses, private charities, and nongovernment organizations. Only the state has the potential to be motivated by the interests of the entire community. This remains true despite laissez-faire attempts to denigrate it as an appropriate agency for addressing social problems with suitable social programs.

For sure, the state most often has been captured by partial interests and has not represented the interests of the entire people. For the state to reach its potential, it therefore must be substantially democratized. It must substantively, and not just in form, represent the interests of the entire society.

Afterword:
Social Impacts of the
Great Recession in Europe
and the United States

The first edition of this book was published in late 2006 during a period of relative economic prosperity and growth in Europe and the United States. Its main thesis was that Europe and the United States shared the status of being high-income capitalist economies but with different social models. Europeans pay high taxes and receive generous social benefits. Americans pay low taxes and receive few social benefits. High-income capitalist economies can economically function with either approach, but with very different social consequences.

Thus, in 2006, a time of relative prosperity, there were clear differences between social conditions in Europe and the United States. Because of intentional government policy, Europe had less income inequality and poverty than the United States. It had less health inequality since all of its citizens had health insurance, unlike in the United States, where 15 percent had no insurance at all and many more had only token insurance. Because 2006 was a year of strong economic growth, both areas had relatively low unemployment rates. But neither had a zero unemployment rate, which would be a rare occurrence for capitalist economies. Both had programs to deliver benefits to the unemployed, but those of Europe were more generous and of more lasting duration.

An underlying view that bridges ideological differences in Europe is that strong social programs and safety nets are prudent investments in social integration and peace. Societies function better if their members are integrated into them with the means, including income, to participate in normal ways. Marginalization of citizens promotes alienation and social breakdown. For that reason, Europeans have embraced social inclusion as a means and goal of social policy.

For historical and cultural reasons, social policy in the United States has been marked by individualism and anti-statism. Each individual, according to the dominant belief, is presumed to be responsible for her or his own welfare. There is a deep suspicion of government action for social purposes. Despite paying much lower taxes than Europeans, Americans complain much more about the taxes they do pay. In the eyes of many Americans, they are absolutely and oppressively overtaxed.

To some extent, the United States compensates for its lack of a developed welfare state with an extensive prison system. Its incarceration rate, many times higher than that of Europe, is the highest in the world. If in Europe there is a commitment to using welfare policies to compensate for the failure of labor markets to provide living-wage employment for all who need it, in the United States those who cannot obtain living-wage employment are forced to adapt to sub-living-wage conditions or inadequate welfare support. Many supplement sub-living-wage incomes with more lucrative profits from a burgeoning drug economy that has moved into the vacuum left in deindustrialized cities. It is a risky survival strategy in which the odds of serving time in prison are high.[1]

THE GREAT RECESSION

The recession began in late summer 2008 in Europe and the United States. By October, it was clear that the contraction in economic activity was much more severe than in previous recessions.[2] It bottomed out in 2009, with the International Monetary Fund estimating contractions of the gross domestic product at -3.9 in the Euro area and -2.5 in the United States. By 2010, economies on both sides of the Atlantic were growing again, although weakly.[3] There had been an acute contraction followed by a long, slow recovery. If there were social consequences of the differences between strong and weak welfare states during periods of relative economic prosperity, there were even stronger differences between them during deep recessions. There was not as much of a social safety net to catch the recession's victims in the United States as in Europe.

Business cycles and unemployment rates are largely mirror images of each other. When an economy is growing, new jobs are created and unemployment decreases; when an economy declines, people are laid off and unemployment rates increase. The Great Recession was no different. Unemployment rates increased in Europe and the United States. In the European Union, the rate increased from 7.1 to 9.5 percent between 2007 and 2009, the year in which the recession bottomed out. In the United States during the same period, it increased from 4.6 to 10.1 percent.[4]

Before the onset of the recession, unemployment at 7.1 percent was significantly higher in Europe than in the United States. Many conservative commentators in the United States blamed the European welfare state for the higher rate, claiming that it undermined the work ethic by providing alternative sources of income.

There is some truth to that argument. When people have income alternatives, they are not so desperate that they will accept any job, no matter how unfavorable its conditions.[5] Put differently, income and, as we have argued throughout this book, social stability depend relatively more on conditions within the labor market in the United States than those in Europe. The more developed European welfare state functions as a more effective shock absorber for failures of labor markets to provide enough living-wage income opportunities. An unemployment rate spike will thus have more serious social consequences in the United States.

Regardless of what the rates were before the recession, by the business-cycle low point in 2009, the U.S. unemployment rate had surpassed that of Europe. The size of the spike in the unemployment rate was thus much larger in the United States—from 4.5 to 10.1 percent versus from 7.5 to 9.4 percent in Europe. The shock to social stability was greater in the United States because of the relatively greater increase in unemployment and because it depended on high employment rates to compensate for weak social programs.

The more direct cause-and-effect link between position in the labor market and life chances in the United States, because of its lack of a strong welfare state, is nowhere more evident than in access to health insurance. The overwhelming majority (69 percent) of those who have health insurance receive it as an employment benefit.[6] For them and usually their dependents, unemployment results in a loss of insurance coverage. To purchase it directly would be prohibitively expensive, especially when income has plummeted. As the recession-induced unemployment rate increased, therefore, so too did the uninsured rate—from 13.9 to 16.7 percent between September 2008 and October 2009.[7] Lack of health insurance in turn aggravated health conditions and increased premature deaths.

The 2010 Health Reform will make it easier for unemployed persons to maintain health insurance coverage. Their drop in income will make them eligible to purchase individual insurance at subsidized rates. The reform, however, will not go far enough to assure complete continuity of their coverage as exists in Europe. What had been provided as an employee benefit they will be required to purchase, and that will be a new expense, however much subsidized, at precisely the time when their income will have significantly declined.

Unemployment was aggravated in the United States by the stock market hit suffered by private retirement accounts—Individual Retirement

Accounts, 401(k)s, and the like. These private defined-contribution retirement accounts that are sensitive to market swings constitute 44 percent
of retirement sources of income in the United States, more than double
the European average.[8] Sharp reductions in their account balances forced
many who were about to retire to delay leaving the labor force. They held
on to labor force positions rather than vacate them, thereby adding to the
pressures driving up the unemployment rate.

The economic downturn thus sent unemployment rates sharply up-
ward in Europe and the United States. However, the standards of living
of the European unemployed suffered much less because of their more
generous income replacement programs and other services such as universal health insurance, which were not affected. Ironically, one of the
features that distinguished the situation in the United States was that it
led to people both being kept from jobs and being trapped within them.
The first were, as in Europe, workers who were laid off because of the economic downturn or new workers entering labor forces with scarce openings. The second, unlike in Europe, were workers who had to delay retirement because the downturn had liquidated substantial values within
their private market-sensitive retirement systems. Those who wanted jobs
couldn't find them, and those who had jobs couldn't leave them to retire,
the situation of the first being in part caused by that of the second.

Notes

NOTE TO THE SECOND EDITION

1. Hendrik Herzberg, "Like, Socialism," *New Yorker*, November 3, 2008.

PREFACE

1. Luís Matías López, "La Cuarta Edad: el gobierno quiere convertir la atención a las personas dependientes, ancianos en su mayoría, en el cuarto pilar del estado de bienestar," *El País* (Madrid), July 25, 2004, Domingo section, 1.
2. Seymour Martin Lipset, *American Exceptionalism: A Double-Edged Sword* (New York: W. W. Norton, 1996), 49.

CHAPTER 1

1. Daniel Bell introduced the concept of postindustrial society to refer to those societies where production of services had supplanted production of physical goods as the dominant economic activity. See Bell, *The Coming of Post-Industrial Society* (New York: Basic Books, 1973).
2. The EU–15 was made up of Belgium, Denmark, Germany, Greece, Italy, Spain, France, Ireland, Luxembourg, the Netherlands, Austria, Portugal, Finland, Sweden, and the United Kingdom. The ten new entrants in 2004 were Cyprus, the Czech Republic, Estonia, Hungary, Latvia, Lithuania, Malta, Poland, Slovakia, and Slovenia.

CHAPTER 2

1. Emile Durkheim, *The Division of Labor in Society* (1893; Glencoe, IL: Free Press, 1964), 79.

2. In the thirteenth century, Thomas Aquinas developed reason, based on Aristotelian logic, to its greatest role within the possibilities of medieval Christianity. He saw reason and faith as complementary gifts of God that could be used together to deepen religious being. Even in the thought of Aquinas, though, reason was constrained by what was believed on the basis of faith. See Thomas Aquinas, *Summa Theologiae: A Concise Translation*, ed. Timothy McDermott (1267–1273; Allen, TX: Christian Classics, 1991).

3. Augustine of Hippo (Saint Augustine), "The Predestination of the Blessed," in *Basic Writings of Saint Augustine*, vol. 1, ed. Whitney J. Oates (New York: Random House, 1948).

4. Augustine's doctrine of predestination did not carry the same implications as John Calvin's sixteenth-century doctrine, which Max Weber interpreted as a central causal component in the development of capitalism in The *Protestant Ethic and the Spirit of Capitalism* (1905; London: Routledge, 1992). For Calvin, success at one's occupational vocation was a sign of grace. Social inequality by implication reflected God's will in unequally distributing grace. Augustine's notion of grace never went so far, though, as to identify goodness with economic success.

5. Augustine of Hippo, *The City of God* (AD 426; New York: Random House, 1993), bk. 19, chap. 13.

6. Augustine, *City of God*, bk. 19, chap. 14.

7. Marc Bloch, *Feudal Society* (Chicago: University of Chicago, 1961); "Feudalism, European," *Encyclopedia of the Social Sciences* (New York: Macmillan, 1933).

CHAPTER 3

1. Thomas Hobbes, *Leviathan* (1651; Cambridge: Cambridge University Press, 1991), 86.

2. "To understand political power aright, and derive it from its original, we must consider what estate all men are naturally in, and that is, a state of perfect freedom . . . [and] a state also of equality . . . born to all the same advantages of Nature." John Locke, *Two Treatises of Government*, ed. Peter Laslett (1690; Cambridge: Cambridge University Press, 1988), bk. 2, chap. 2, sec. 4.

3. Friedrich Nietzsche, *The Will to Power*, trans. Walter Kaufmann and R. J. Hollingdale (1901; New York: Random House, 1967), 479. Nietzsche's reference is to Auguste Comte, the founder of sociology, who advocated that sociologists, armed with scientific understanding of societies, should form a sociocracy to guide them. Comte, *System of Positive Polity* (1851–1854; Dorset, UK: Thoemmes Continuum, 2002).

4. Emile Durkheim, *The Division of Labor in Society*, trans. George Simpson (1893; New York: Free Press, 1964), 377.

5. Hobbes, *Leviathan*, 90.

6. Jean-Jacques Rousseau, *Discourse on the Origin of Inequality* (1755; Indianapolis, IN: Hackett Publishing, 1992).

7. "The more deeply we go back into history, the more does the individual, and hence also the producing individual, appear as dependent, as belonging to a greater whole." Karl Marx, *Grundrisse* (1857–1858; Middlesex, UK: Penguin), 84. The communal origins of humans are also developed by Frederick Engels in *The Origin of the Family, Private Property and the State* (1884; Moscow: Progress Publishers, 1948).

8. "Let us then suppose the mind to be, as we say, white paper, void of all characters, without any ideas: How comes it to be furnished? . . . To this I answer, in one word, from experience." John Locke, *An Essay Concerning Human Understanding* (1690; Oxford: Oxford University Press, 1979), bk. 2, chap. 1, sec. 2.

9. A variation of the argument is to allege that without unequal occupational rewards, individuals will not be motivated to go through advanced educational training. That position was classically articulated in Kingsley Davis and Wilbert Moore, "Some Principles of Stratification," *American Sociological Review* 10 (1945): 242–49.

10. Max Weber, *The Protestant Ethic and the Spirit of Capitalism* (1905; London: Routledge, 1992).

11. Max Weber, "Class, Status, Party," in *From Max Weber: Essays in Sociology*, trans. and ed. Hans H. Gerth and C. Wright Mills (New York: Oxford University Press, 1946).

12. Guillermo Bonfil Batalla, *México Profundo* (Mexico City: Grijalbo, 1990).

13. Jean-Jacques Rousseau, *The Social Contract* (1762; New York: Hafner, 1951), 5.

14. Max Weber, "Politics as a Vocation," in *From Max Weber*, 79.

15. Wilhelm Reich, "Dialectical Materialism and Psychoanalysis," *Studies on the Left* (July–August 1966), orig. pub. in 1929.

16. Sigmund Freud, *Civilization and Its Discontents* (New York: Jonathan Cape, 1930).

17. Sigmund Freud, "Why War?" in *The Standard Edition of the Complete Psychological Works of Sigmund Freud*, vol. 22, ed. and trans. James Strachey (1933; London: Hogarth, 1964).

18. Albert Einstein, "Why Socialism?" *Monthly Review*, May 1949.

CHAPTER 4

1. Contemporary use of the concept of decommodification is most associated with Gøsta Esping-Andersen's pioneering study, *The Three Worlds of Welfare Capitalism* (Princeton, NJ: Princeton University Press, 1990). Esping-Andersen states that he "came to the concept of de-commodification because of multiple influences. One— and the most certain—came from reading Polanyi's *The Great Transformation*. Another influence behind the concept was Claus Offe. But one thing is certain, namely that the concept (as far as I am concerned) didn't come out of reading Marx, at least not in any direct way," (communication to the author, October 3, 2005). Claus Offe earlier had mentioned the concept in his *Strukturprobleme des kapitalistischen Staates*

(Frankfurt: Suhrkamp, 1972), 40. For Offe, however, the Marxian roots of the concept are more direct. He states that he "introduced the concept, following, but also revising Marx," (communication to the author, October 7, 2005). In either case, indirect or direct, the influence of Marx is clear.

2. The description that follows summarizes Marx's analysis in *Capital*, vol. 1 (1867; Moscow: Progress Publishers, n.d.).

3. Market fetishism is most developed by Marx in an eleven-page section, "The Fetishism of Commodities and the Secret Thereof" in *Capital*, vol. 1. Earlier, he applied the same idea to worker alienation. "Just as in religion the spontaneous activity of the human imagination, of the human brain and the human heart, operates independently of the individual—that is, operates on him as an alien, divine or diabolical activity—in the same way the worker's activity is not his spontaneous activity. It belongs to another; it is the loss of the self." Karl Marx, *Economic and Philosophic Manuscripts of 1844* (1844; Moscow: Progress Publishers, 1959), 69.

4. "Areas of social life that have been decommodified by welfare state interventions can be developed, through political struggle, into relatively autonomous subsystems of life oriented to the production and distribution of use-values." Claus Offe, *Contradictions of the Welfare State* (Cambridge, MA: MIT Press, 1984), 265.

CHAPTER 5

1. In other hands the term *liberal* continues to be used closer to its original nineteenth-century laissez-faire meaning. That is the case in parts of Europe, including Germany. That is also the case in Latin America, where *neoliberalism* is taken to be the doctrine advocating free markets and privatization of state industries.

2. Edmund Burke, *Reflections on the Revolution in France* (1790; New York: Oxford University Press, 1999).

3. Hans H. Gerth and C. Wright Mills, *Character and Social Structure* (New York: Harcourt Brace, 1953).

4. Karl Mannheim, *Ideology and Utopia*, trans. Louis Wirth and Edward Shils (New York: Harcourt, Brace & World, 1936), 233.

5. Cf.: "Conservatism in Europe and Canada, derived from the historic alliance of church and government, is associated with the emergence of the welfare state. . . . What Europeans have called 'liberalism,' Americans refer to as 'conservatism': a deeply anti-statist doctrine emphasizing the virtues of laissez-faire." Seymour Martin Lipset, *American Exceptionalism: A Double-Edged Sword* (New York: W. W. Norton, 1996), 35–36.

6. For a discussion of the evolution of one mainstream European socialist party's ideology, see "125 Años de Socialismo Español," Temas Para El Debate, nos. 117–118 (August–September, 2004).

7. For a description of how American conservatives have successfully made liberalism and liberals objects of hatred in the eyes of many ordinary citizens who would benefit from liberal policies, see Thomas Frank, *What's the Matter with Kansas?* (New York: Henry Holt, 2004).

CHAPTER 6

1. See Gøsta Esping-Andersen, prologue to *Política Social: Una Introducción*, by Teresa Montagut (Barcelona: Editorial Ariel, 2000), 11.

2. Some authors see the welfare state as being intimately related to democracy, arguing that it arose because politicians offered it to citizens in return for votes. Where there is democracy there can be a welfare state. Where there is no democracy, there cannot be one. By this line of reasoning, the Spanish welfare state only developed in 1978 after the end of the fascist Franco government despite there being extensive social programs during the fascist period. Similarly, by this line of reasoning, the extensive social programs that existed in Eastern Europe and the Soviet Union before 1989 did not constitute a welfare state if those countries were not judged to have been democratic. The problem with linking the welfare state and democracy is that if the core of the concept of the welfare state has to do with whether a government takes on as a central responsibility developing a set of social programs to assure the welfare of its citizens, then that can occur under multiple political forms. A benevolent dictatorship could constitute a welfare state by virtue of its extensive generous social programs. See Montagut, *Política Social*, 44 and 169; and Margarita Garcia Padilla, "Historia de la Acción Social: Seguridad Social y Asistencia (1939–1975)," in *Historia de la acción social pública en España: Beneficia y Previsión* (Madrid: Ministerio de Trabajo y Seguridad Social, 1990).

3. William Smith, *A Dictionary of Greek and Roman Antiquities* (London: John Murray, 1875), 548.

4. "What is distinctive about American social welfare practice is not the level of spending but the source." Jacob S. Hacker, *The Divided Welfare State: The Battle over Public and Private Social Benefits in the United States* (Cambridge: Cambridge University Press, 2002), 7.

5. In the United States, the term *social inclusion* occasionally appears in policy discussions—not nearly as much as in European discussions—though with only liberals seeming to find the concept at all useful. In the 1990s there was a fleeting liberal attempt to develop on American soil a parallel version of the European concerns with social inclusion, cohesion, and solidarity under the name of communitarianism. See, for example, Amitai Etzioni, *The Spirit of Community: The Reinvention of American Society* (New York: Touchstone, 1993). Its endorsers included social scientists and some leading Democratic Party political figures, such as former president Bill Clinton. The concept of communitarianism never took deep hold, though, and soon passed out of the political discourse.

American conservatives never embraced the goal of social inclusion for two reasons. First, they, unlike European conservatives, are more grounded in the philosophy of individualistic freedom than in upholding the traditional community. Second, they are much more anti-statist than European conservatives and thus loath to use the state to promote policies such as social inclusion.

6. For a comprehensive discussion of American exceptionalism, see Seymour Martin Lipset, *American Exceptionalism: A Double-Edged Sword* (New York: W. W. Norton, 1996). Lipset (292) cites Marx in *Capital*, vol. 1 (1867; Moscow: Progress Publishers, n.d.), 8, that "the more advanced country shows the less developed the image of their future" to imply that Europe will eventually shed its "post-

feudal" characteristics; for example, the noblesse oblige stance of its upper classes in supporting a welfare state, and become more like the United States. The citation from Marx, though, could as easily be interpreted to mean that the welfare state is the harbinger of future socialism—not a post-feudal leftover—and that eventually the United States will become more like Europe in that respect.

7. Lewis Hartz, *The Liberal Tradition in America* (New York: Harcourt, Brace & World, 1955).

8. I have discussed the differences between capitalist development in the United States and Mexico in chapter 4 of *After the Fifth Sun: Class and Race in North America* (Englewood Cliffs, NJ: Prentice Hall, 1994).

9. Max Weber, *The Protestant Ethic and the Spirit of Capitalism* (1905; New York: Scribner's, 1948).

10. See Emile Durkheim, *The Division of Labor in Society*, trans. George Simpson (1893; Glencoe, IL: Free Press, 1964), and *Suicide*, trans. J. A. Spaulding and George Simpson (1895; Glencoe, IL: Free Press, 1964).

11. "America, then, exhibits in her social state an extraordinary phenomenon. Men are there seen on a greater equality in point of fortune and intellect, or, in other words, more equal in their strength, than in any other country of the world, or in any age of which history has preserved the remembrance." Tocqueville also noted about the United States, "I know of no country, indeed, where the love of money has taken stronger hold on the affections of men and where a profounder contempt is expressed for the theory of the permanent equality of property." Alexis de Tocqueville, *Democracy in America*, vol. 1 (1835; New York: Bantam, 2000), chap. 3.

12. Seymour Martin Lipset and Noah M. Meltz, *The Paradox of American Unionism* (Ithaca, NY: ILR Press of Cornell University Press, 2004), 97.

13. See Theda Skocpol, *Protecting Soldiers and Mothers: The Political Origins of Social Policy in the United States* (Cambridge, MA: Harvard University Press, 1992).

14. The term *state* in the American context refers to provincial governments rather than the national or city governments, whereas in Europe it refers to government as a whole.

15. Frances Fox Piven and Richard A. Cloward, *Regulating the Poor: The Functions of Public Welfare* (1971; New York: Vintage, 1993).

16. Paul Pierson, *Dismantling the Welfare State? Reagan, Thatcher, and the Politics of Retrenchment* (Cambridge: Cambridge University Press, 1994); Jill Quadagno, "Social Security Policy and the Entitlement Debate: The New American Exceptionalism," in *Social Policy and the Conservative Agenda*, ed. Clarence Y. H. Lo and Michael Schwartz (Malden, MA: Blackwell Publishers, 1998).

CHAPTER 7

1. Editorial, "Let Market Dictate Wages," *Hartford Courant*, February 18, 2004.

2. The guiding principles of American approaches are less likely to be attached to the names of particular theorists than are European ones. There are no comparably recognizable names to Marx or Durkheim. Rather, the justifications are more based upon pragmatic social adaptation to experienced market realities than on specific theories. If the American Declaration of Independence can start with the phrase, "We hold these truths to be self-evident," implicit American social policy

can proceed from a supposedly self-evident faith in the market. European thinking is less likely to employ the pragmatic notion that a truth can be self-evident. Its truths and guiding principles are more likely to require logical demonstration, hence the relatively greater importance of particular social thinkers in guiding the development of its approaches.

3. Gøsta Esping-Andersen, *The Three Worlds of Welfare Capitalism* (Princeton, NJ: Princeton University Press, 1990), 37.

4. Kees Van Kersbergen, *Social Capitalism: A Study of Christian Democracy and the Welfare State* (London: Routledge, 1995), 15.

5. I am here employing the methodology of Max Weber in describing abstract, opposing ideal types of social policies. As such these ideal types exist in their purity nowhere. The purpose of ideal types is not to provide exact descriptions of actually occurring realities but rather to facilitate thinking and research, to highlight underlying directions of policy choices. "The more sharply and precisely the ideal type has been constructed, thus the more abstract and unrealistic in this sense it is, the better it is able to perform its functions in formulating terminology, classifications, and hypotheses." See Max Weber, *Economy and Society* (1922; New York: Bedminster Press, 1968), 21.

Ideal types also provide referents—conceptual mental rulers so to speak—for measuring and comparing the differences between actual realities. We can measure the extent to which the social policies of the United States and the various countries of Europe are closer to one or the other ideal-type poles and thus differ from each other. All national policies in actuality incorporate different mixes of the policy ingredients, with these on balance ending up closer to one or the other of the ideal-type poles.

6. Emile Durkheim, *The Division of Labor in Society* (1893; New York: Free Press, 1964).

7. Esping-Andersen, *Three Worlds of Welfare Capitalism*. While Esping-Andersen distinguishes the Christian democratic—he uses the label *corporatist*—from the social democratic model, he does not distinguish conservative and liberal varieties, instead preferring to include both under the label *liberal*. I believe that approach is confusing on two counts. First, he uses *liberal* in its mid-nineteenth-century sense in which it indicated the laissez-faire state, when the current meaning of *liberal*, at least in the United States, has changed. Contemporary U.S. liberals embrace the necessity of a more economically and socially activist state. Second, within his category of liberal welfare regimes, he includes those of the United States, Canada, and the United Kingdom, despite there being significant social benefit outcome differences between the first and the latter two. I therefore believe that it makes more sense to distinguish conservative and liberal ideological approaches to the welfare state using the contemporary meanings of those terms.

8. Van Kersbergen, *Social Capitalism*, 98.

9. Teresa Montagut, *Política Social: Una Introducción* (Barcelona: Editorial Ariel, 2000), 56.

CHAPTER 8

1. Jean-Jacques Rousseau, *The Social Contract* (1762; New York: Hafner, 1951), 46.

2. Frederick Engels, *Anti-Duhring* (1878; Moscow: Progress Publishers, 1969), 123.

3. OECD, *Government at a Glance 2009*, www.oecd.org/document/33/0,3343 ,en_2649_33735_43714657_1_1_1_1,00.html#es (accessed March 31, 2010).

4. U.S. Bureau of the Census, *Statistical Abstract of the United States 2010* (Washington, DC: U.S. Government Printing Office), table 648.

5. "It is clear that the salaries and bonus packages available in the United States far exceed those paid to top executives in most European countries." The pay differences are not based on performance differences. Rather, "The evidence remains that many European executives prefer living and working in Europe for non-monetary reasons." See Deanne Julius, "U.S. Economic Power: Waxing or Waning?" *Harvard International Review* 26, no. 4 (Winter 2005).

6. Bureau of Labor Statistics, "Employer Costs for Employee Compensation Summary," news release, March 10, 2010, www.bls.gov/news.release/pdf/ecec .pdf (accessed April 1, 2010).

7. Karl Marx, "Critique of the Gotha Programme," in *Karl Marx and Frederick Engels, Selected Works in Three Volumes* (1875; Moscow: Progress Publishers, 1970).

CHAPTER 9

1. U.S. Department of Health and Human Services, "The 2009 HHS Poverty Guidelines," http://aspe.hhs.gov/poverty/09poverty.shtml (accessed April 3, 2010).

2. Mollie Orshansky, "Children of the Poor," *Social Security Bulletin* 26, no. 7 (July 1963).

3. Orshansky, "Children of the Poor," 8.

4. Jared Bernstein, "Who's Poor? Don't Ask the Census Bureau," *New York Times*, September 26, 2003, 1.

5. Carmen DeNavas-Walt, Bernadette D. Proctor, and Jessica C. Smith, Current Population Reports, Series P60-236RV, *Income, Poverty and Health Insurance in the United States 2008* (Washington, DC: U.S. Government Printing Office, 2009), table B-1.

6. "Following the introduction of the Amsterdam Treaty (Articles 136 and 137) of the fight against social exclusion among the Union objectives, the Lisbon European Council of March 2000 asked Member States and the European Commission to take steps to make a decisive impact on the eradication of poverty by 2010. Building a more inclusive European Union was thus considered as an essential element in achieving the Union's ten year strategic goal of sustained economic growth, more and better jobs and greater social cohesion." See "Social Inclusion," European Commission, http://europa.eu.int/comm/employment_social/ social_inclusion/index_en.htm.

7. Current Population Reports, Series P60-232, *The Effect of Taxes and Transfers on Income and Poverty in the United States: 2005* (Washington, DC: U.S. Government Printing Office, 2007), table 6.

8. Historical context as well as ideological orientation affects poverty policy. In the liberal climate of the late 1960s and early 1970s, conservative Republican presi-

dent Richard M. Nixon advocated expansion of liberal state transfer programs to fight poverty, while in the more conservative climate of the middle 1990s, liberal Democratic president Bill Clinton endorsed a conservative cutback of those same programs.

CHAPTER 10

1. See Karl Polanyi, *The Great Transformation* (1944; Boston: Beacon Press, 1957).

2. Karl Marx, *Capital*, vol. 1 (1867; Moscow: Progress Publishers, n.d.), chaps. 27–28.

3. Peter Kolchin, *American Slavery: 1619–1877* (New York: Hill and Wang, 1993), 8.

4. Adam Smith, *The Wealth of Nations* (1776; Harmondsworth, UK: Penguin, 1982), 158.

5. For Durkheim's discussions of anomie, see *The Division of Labor in Society* (1893; Glencoe, IL: Free Press, 1964), and *Suicide* (1897; Glencoe, IL: Free Press, 1964).

6. M. Harvey Brenner, *Estimating the Social Costs of National Economic Policy* (Washington, DC: U.S. Congress Joint Economic Committee, 1976); M. Harvey Brenner, "Commentary: Economic Growth Is the Basis of Mortality Decline in the 20th Century—Experience of the United States 1901–2000," *International Journal of Epidemiology* 34, no. 6 (December 2005): 1214–21; Claes-Goran Stefansson, "Long-Term Unemployment and Mortality in Sweden, 1980–1986," *Social Science and Medicine* 32, no. 4 (1991): 419–23.

7. The controversy, though, is contradictory given the conservative principle that hard work in and of itself is virtuous. As Max Weber famously argued in *The Protestant Ethic and the Spirit of Capitalism*, the Protestant work ethic began because Luther believed that God intended for individuals to work hard at their callings. Luther did not qualify the belief by adding that hard work was only important if it could be performed profitably. If it is believed that hard work has a redeeming personal and social value regardless of whether it is performed profitably, then the laissez-faire principle has to give way so that work can be created that may not be profitable. The fallback principle then becomes creating work that is useful to the person or society—artistic creations that add beauty to schools and childcare centers, cleaning debris from the sides of roads, or crosswalk guards for school children are examples of work that is useful but not profitable.

CHAPTER 11

1. Max Weber, "Bureaucracy," in *From Max Weber: Essays in Sociology*, trans. and ed. Hans H. Gerth and C. Wright Mills (New York: Oxford University Press, 1958), 196–98, and *The Protestant Ethic and the Spirit of Capitalism* (1905; London: Routledge, 1992), 9.

2. See Anne Hélène Gauthier, *The State and the Family: A Comparative Analysis of Family Policies in Industrialized Countries* (Oxford: Clarendon Press, 1996), 16ff. Later, twentieth-century neo-Malthusians would argue that the opposite problem was occurring in developing societies: birth rates were too high, causing the need

for programs to lower them. See, for example, William Barclay, Joseph Enright, and Reid T. Reynolds, "Population Control in the Third World," *NACLA Newsletter* 4, no. 8 (December 1970); Bonnie Mass, *Population Target: The Political Economy of Population Control in Latin America* (Brampton, ON: Charters, 1976).

3. Rebecca Ray, Janet C. Gornick, and John Schmitt, "Parental Leave Policies in 21 Countries Assessing Generosity and Gender Equality" (Washington, DC: Center for Economic and Policy Research, 2008), 2.

4. Ray, Gornick, and Schmitt, "Parental Leave Policies," 2.

5. June Lawler Dye, "Fertility of American Women: June 2004," *Current Population Reports*, P20–555 (Washington, DC: U.S. Census Bureau, 2005), fig. 2.

6. Sheila B. Kamerman and Shirley Gatenio, "Tax Day: How Do America's Child Benefits Compare?" The Clearinghouse on International Developments in Child, Youth and Family Policies Issue Brief, Spring 2002.

7. Emile Durkheim, *The Division of Labor in Society* (1893; Glencoe, IL: Free Press, 1964), bk. 3, chap. 2, "The Forced Division of Labor."

8. Durkheim, *The Division of Labor*, 378.

9. A centerpiece of conservative president George W. Bush's tax agenda in the United States was to abolish taxes on inherited wealth, which are derisively referred to as death taxes.

10. Pierre Bourdieu, *Practical Reason* (Stanford, CA: Stanford University Press, 1998), 19.

11. Seymour Martin Lipset, *American Exceptionalism: A Double-Edged Sword* (New York: W. W. Norton, 1996), 22.

12. OECD, *Education at a Glance 2009*, www.oecd.org/document/24/0,3343 ,en_2649_39263238_43586328_1_1_1_1,00.html (accessed April 7, 2010).

13. Lipset, *American Exceptionalism*, 82.

CHAPTER 12

1. See Robin Blackburn, *Banking on Death; or, Investing in Life: The History and Future of Pensions* (London: Verso, 2002), 79; Jacob S. Hacker, *The Great Risk Shift: The New Economic Insecurity and the Decline of the American Dream*, rev. ed. (New York: Oxford University Press, 2008), 120; and Teresa Ghilarducci, *When I'm Sixty-four: The Plot against Pensions and the Plan to Save Them* (Princeton, NJ: Princeton University Press, 2008), 130.

2. That did not stop President George W. Bush from favorably citing the Chilean example in 2004 in his campaign to partially privatize Social Security through the creation of defined-contribution accounts.

3. Willem Adema and Maxine Ladaique, "How Expensive Is the Welfare State?" OECD Social, Employment and Migration Working Papers No. 92 (Paris: OECD, 2009), chart 4.3.

4. European Commission, Eurostat, http://nui.epp.eurostat.ec.europa.eu/nui/ show.do?dataset=ilc_pnp2&lang=en (accessed April 7, 2010); U.S. Bureau of the Census, *Statistical Abstract of the United States 2009* (Washington, DC: U.S. Government Printing Office, 2009), table 626.

CHAPTER 13

1. World Health Organization, *World Health Report 2000* (Geneva: World Health Organization, 2000), 24.

2. Institute of Medicine of the National Academies, *Insuring America's Health* (Washington, DC: National Academies Press, 2004), 8.

3. Chris L. Peterson and Rachel Burton, "U.S. Health Care Spending: Comparison with Other OECD Countries," *Congressional Research Service*, September 17, 2007, table 2.

4. The World Health Organization has not repeated the ranking in its subsequent reports.

5. Cited in Richard Freeman, *The Politics of Health in Europe* (Manchester: Manchester University Press, 2000), 26.

6. See Freeman, *The Politics of Health in Europe*, 5; and Robert H. Blank and Viola Burau, *Comparative Health Policy* (Hampshire, UK: Palgrave Macmillan, 2004), 22.

7. World Health Organization, *World Health Report 2000*, 24.

8. Vicente Navarro, "Luces y sombras de la reforma sanitaria de Obama," *Rebelión*, March 27, 2010, www.rebelion.org.

CHAPTER 14

1. "There exists a growing conviction over the necessity that the European Union convert itself into a type of federation or confederation of states, in a certain way, that is closer to the present federal political system of the United States." Guillermo de la Dehesa, *¿Quo vadis Europa? Por qué la Unión Europea sigue creciendo más lentamente que Estados Unidos* (Madrid: Alianza Editorial, 2004), 10. Jeremy Rifkin makes a similar argument in *The European Dream: How Europe's Vision of the Future Is Quietly Eclipsing the American Dream* (New York: Tarcher/Penguin, 2004).

2. Max Weber, "Politics as a Vocation," in *From Max Weber: Essays in Sociology*, trans. and ed. Hans H. Gerth and C. Wright Mills (New York: Oxford University Press, 1946).

3. Ruth Wodak and Maria Sedlak, "'We Demand That the Foreigners Adapt to Our Life Style': Political Discourse on Immigration Laws in Austria and the United Kingdom," in *Combating Racial Discrimination: Affirmative Action as a Model for Europe*, ed. Erna Appelt and Monika Jarosch (Oxford: Berg, 2000), 219.

4. Immigrant populations are made up of three components: authorized immigrants, illegal or undocumented immigrants, and naturalized citizens. In addition, a noncitizen resident population can also contain temporary immigrants such as guest workers and students. These distinctions must be kept in mind when examining immigration statistics. Figures on noncitizen residents, for example, understate the scale of immigration since they do not include those immigrants who have become naturalized citizens.

5. Calculated on the basis of data in European Commission, *European Social Statistics: Migration* (Luxembourg: Office for Official Publication of the European Communities, 2002), 48, table E-2.

6. Calculated from information in Jean-Christophe Dumont and Georges Le-maître, "Counting Immigrants and Expatriates: A New Perspective," OECD, Social, Employment and Migration Working Papers (Paris: OECD, 2010), table A-1.

7. The increase in illegal immigration provoked by NAFTA occurred despite the proclamations of the treaty's proponents and architects that it would result in the opposite. The proponents argued, more out of political necessity than on the basis of sound analysis, that NAFTA would so stimulate the Mexican economy that enough new jobs would be created so that workers would not need to migrate in search of work. This was part of a disinguous campaign to promote NAFTA that I have discussed in *Class and Race Formation in North America* (Toronto: University of Toronto Press, 2009), 106–9.

8. Jennifer Van Hook and Frank D. Bean, "Estimating Unauthorized Mexican Migration to the United States: Issues and Results," in U.S. Commission on Immigration Reform, *The Binational Study of Migration Between Mexico and the United States*, vol. 2 (1997); Frank D. Bean, Jennifer Van Hook, and Karen Woodrow-Lafield, "Estimates of Numbers of Unauthorized Migrants Residing in the United States" (Washington, DC: Pew Hispanic Center, Pew Charitable Trusts, 2002).

9. "According to the Superior Agrarian Court, 30 percent of cultivated lands are controlled by drug cartels." Editorial, "Emiliano Zapata y la ruina del campo," *La Jornada* (Mexico City), April 10, 2010.

10. "Fear of Captivity," *The Economist*, June 17, 2004.

11. Editorial, "CEESP: ¿Más Reformas Estructurales?" *La Jornada* (Mexico City), April 19, 2010.

12. Instituto Nacional de Estadística Geografía e Informática (INEGI), *XI Censo General de Población y Vivienda, 1990* (Aguascalientes: INEGI, 1992); Instituto Nacional Estadística (INE), *Encuestas de Población Activa*, cited in Teresa Montagut, *Política Social: Una Introducción* (Barcelona: Editorial Ariel, 2000), 152.

13. These are discussed by Weber in *Economy and Society* (New York: Bedminster Press, 1968), especially 1056–69, and *General Economic History*, trans. Frank H. Knight (New York: Dover, 2003).

14. Mary Patrice Erdmans, *The Grasininski Girls: The Choices They Had and the Choices They Made* (Athens: Ohio University Press, 2005), 60.

15. Erdmans, *Grasininski Girls*, 59.

16. See Han Entzinger and Renske Biezeveld, "Benchmarking in Immigrant Integration," Report for the European Commission (Rotterdam: European Research Centre on Migration and Ethnic Relations at Erasmus University, 2003), www.europa.eu.int/comm/justice_home/doc_centre/immigration/studies/docs/benchmarking_final_en.pdf.

17. Executive Order 11246 (Lyndon Baines Johnson, September 24, 1965), www.dol.gov/esa/regs/statutes/ofccp/eo11246.htm.

CHAPTER 15

1. Tom W. Smith, "Public Attitudes toward the Regulation of Firearms" (Chicago: National Opinion Research Center, 2007), fig. 2.

2. The perception of American violence is worse than the reality. Homicide rates have been decreasing, and most homicide victims are killed by people they know, not by random street assailants. Nevertheless, perceptions, however distorted, reflect social realities. In this case, the reality is that it is believable, even if exaggerated, that there is extensive violence in American society.

3. U.S. Bureau of Justice Statistics, "Prisoners in 2008," appendix table 14, http://bjs.ojp.usdoj.gov/index.cfm?ty=pbdetail&iid=1763 (accessed April 12, 2010).

AFTERWORD

1. For an excellent ethnographic description of how individuals supplement formal sub-living-wage incomes with more lucrative profits from the illicit informal drug market, see Tim Black, *When a Heart Turns Rock Solid: The Lives of Three Puerto Rican Brothers On and Off the Streets* (New York: Pantheon, 2009).

2. The technical definition of a recession is when the gross domestic product—the total value of goods and services produced—declines for two quarters or six months. Surprisingly there is no technical definition for what constitutes an economic depression. The only commonly assumed meaning is that it is more serious than a recession. Ironically, in the 1920s the meanings were often reversed, with depression being taken to be a slight dip in economic activity that was not dangerous to the overall economies, while recessions were taken to be serious declines in production.

3. International Monetary Fund, *World Economic Outlook Update*, January 26, 2010, table 1.1, www.imf.org/external/pubs/ft/weo/2010/update/01/index.htm#tbl1 (accessed March 23, 2010).

4. OECD, "Harmonised Unemployment Rates News Release: January 2010," www.oecd.org/dataoecd/20/21/44746304.pdf (accessed March 3, 2010).

5. Many who are counted as fully employed in the United States are actually part-time employees. In Europe there are relatively fewer part-time employees counted as part of the employed population.

6. Carmen DeNavas-Walt, Bernadette D. Proctor, and Jessica C. Smith, U.S. Census Bureau, Current Population Reports, P60-236, *Income, Poverty, and Health Insurance Coverage in the United States: 2008* (Washington, DC: U.S. Government Printing Office, 2009), 20.

7. Elizabeth Mendes, "Percentage of Uninsured Adults in U.S. Remains Elevated," *Gallup Poll*, March 17, 2010, www.gallup.com/poll/126791/Percentage-Uninsured-Adults-Remains-Elevated.aspx (accessed March 17, 2010).

8. OECD, *Pensions at a Glance: Retirement-Income Systems in OECD Countries* (Paris: OECD, 2009). See also, Catherine Rampell and Matthew Saltmarsh, "A Reluctance to Retire Means Fewer Openings," *New York Times*, September 2, 2009.

Bibliography

2009 Annual Report of the Boards of Trustees of the Federal Hospital Insurance and Federal Supplementary Medical Insurance Trust Funds. www.cms.hhs .gov/ReportsTrustFunds/downloads/tr2009.pdf (accessed March 29, 2010).

Adema, Willem, and Maxine Ladaique. "How Expensive Is the Welfare State?" OECD Social, Employment and Migration Working Papers No. 92. Paris: OECD, 2009.

Alcock, Pete, and Gary Craig, eds. *International Social Policy*. Hampshire, UK: Palgrave, 2001.

Alvarez, Lizette. "Nagging Pain in Britain: How to Find a Dentist." *New York Times*, August 12, 2003.

Appelt, Erna, and Monika Jarosch, eds. *Combating Racial Discrimination: Affirmative Action as a Model for Europe*. Oxford: Berg, 2000.

Aquinas, Thomas. *Summa Theologiae: A Concise Translation*. 1267–1273. Edited by Timothy McDermott. Allen, TX: Christian Classics, 1991.

Aristotle. *The Politics*. 350 BC. London: Penguin, 1992.

Augustine of Hippo (Saint Augustine). *The City of God*. AD 426. Translated by Marcus Dods. New York: Random House, 1993.

———. "The Predestination of the Blessed." In *Basic Writings of Saint Augustine*, vol. 1, edited by Whitney J. Oates. New York: Random House, 1948.

Bachu, Amara, and Martin O'Connell. "Fertility of American Women: June 2000." *Current Population Reports*, P20–543. Washington, DC: U.S. Census Bureau, 2001.

Barclay, William, Joseph Enright, and Reid T. Reynolds. "Population Control in the Third World." *NACLA Newsletter* 4, no. 8 (December 1970).

Barnes, Harry Elmer, ed. *An Introduction to the History of Sociology*. Chicago: University of Chicago Press, 1948.

Bean, Frank D., Jennifer Van Hook, and Karen Woodrow-Lafield. "Estimates of Numbers of Unauthorized Migrants Residing in the United States." Washington, DC: Pew Hispanic Center, Pew Charitable Trusts, 2002.

Bell, Daniel. *The Coming of Post-Industrial Society*. New York: Basic Books, 1973.

Bernstein, Jared. "Who's Poor? Don't Ask the Census Bureau." *New York Times*, September 26, 2003, 1.

Black, Tim. *When a Heart Turns Rock Solid: The Lives of Three Puerto Rican Brothers On and Off the Streets*. New York: Pantheon, 2009.

Blackburn, Robin. *Banking on Death; or, Investing in Life: The History and Future of Pensions*. London: Verso, 2002.

Blank, Robert H., and Viola Burau. *Comparative Health Policy*. Hampshire, UK: Palgrave Macmillan, 2004.

Bloch, Marc. "Feudalism, European." *Encyclopedia of the Social Sciences*. New York: Macmillan, 1933.

———. *Feudal Society*. 2 vols. Translated by L. A. Manyon. Chicago: University of Chicago Press, 1961.

Bonfil Batalla, Guillermo. *México Profundo*. Mexico City: Grijalbo, 1990.

Bourdieu, Pierre. *Practical Reason*. Stanford, CA: Stanford University Press, 1998.

Brenner, M. Harvey. "Commentary: Economic Growth Is the Basis of Mortality Decline in the 20th Century—Experience of the United States 1901–2000." *International Journal of Epidemiology* 34, no. 6 (December 2005): 1214–21.

———. *Estimating the Social Costs of National Economic Policy*. Washington, DC: U.S. Congress Joint Economic Committee, 1976.

Brown, Ian T., and Christopher Khoury. "In OECD Countries, Universal Healthcare Gets High Marks." Gallup Poll, August 20, 2009.

Brown, Peter. *The Rise of Western Christendom*. 2nd ed. Oxford: Blackwell, 2003.

Burke, Edmund. *Reflections on the Revolution in France*. 1790. New York: Oxford University Press, 1999.

Burns, J. Patout. "Predestination." *Encyclopedia of Early Christianity*, edited by Everett Ferguson. New York: Garland, 1990.

"CEESP: ¿Más Reformas Estructurales?" Editorial. *La Jornada* (Mexico City), April 19, 2010.

Comte, Auguste. *System of Positive Polity*. 1851–1854. Translated by John Henry Bridges et al. Dorset, UK: Thoemmes Continuum, 2002.

Congressional Budget Office. "Summary of Preliminary Analysis of Health and Revenue Provisions of Reconciliation Legislation Combined with H.R. 3590 as Passed by the Senate." Letter to Speaker of the House Nancy Pelosi, March 18, 2010.

Current Population Reports. Series P60-232, *The Effect of Taxes and Transfers on Income and Poverty in the United States: 2005*. Washington, DC: U.S. Government Printing Office, 2007.

Davis, Kingsley, and Wilbert Moore. "Some Principles of Stratification." *American Sociological Review* 10 (1945): 242–49.

de la Dehesa, Guillermo. *¿Quo vadis Europa? Por qué la Unión Europea sigue creciendo más lentamente que Estados Unidos*. Madrid: Alianza Editorial, 2004.

DeNavas-Walt, Carmen, Bernadette D. Proctor, and Jessica C. Smith. U.S. Census Bureau, Current Population Reports, P60-236, *Income, Poverty, and Health Insurance Coverage in the United States, 2008*. Washington, DC: U.S. Government Printing Office, 2009.

———. U.S. Census Bureau, Current Population Reports, Series P60-236RV, *Income, Poverty and Health Insurance in the United States, 2008*. Washington, DC: U.S. Government Printing Office, 2009. Table B-1.

Drier, Peter. "The United States in Comparative Perspective." *Contexts* 6, no. 3 (Summer 2007): 38–46.

Dumont, Jean-Christophe, and Georges Lemaître. "Counting Immigrants and Expatriates: A New Perspective." OECD, Social, Employment and Migration Working Papers. Paris: OECD, 2010.

Durkheim, Emile. *The Division of Labor in Society.* 1893. Translated by George Simpson. Glencoe, IL: Free Press, 1964.

———. *Suicide.* 1895. Translated by J. A. Spaulding and George Simpson. Glencoe, IL: Free Press, 1964.

Dye, June Lawler. "Fertility of American Women: June 2004." Current Population Reports, P20–555. Washington, DC: U.S. Census Bureau, 2005.

Einstein, Albert. "Why Socialism?" *Monthly Review*, May 1949.

"Emiliano Zapata y la ruina del campo." Editorial. *La Jornada* (Mexico City), April 10, 2010.

Engels, Frederick. *Anti-Duhring.* 1878. Moscow: Progress Publishers, 1969.

———. *The Origin of the Family, Private Property and the State.* 1884. Translated by Alick West. Moscow: Progress Publishers, 1948.

Entzinger, Han, and Renske Biezeveld. "Benchmarking in Immigrant Integration." Report for the European Commission, 2003. http://europa.eu.int/comm/justice_home/funding/doc/study_indicators_integration.pdf.

Erdmans, Mary Patrice. *The Grasininski Girls: The Choices They Had and the Choices They Made.* Athens: Ohio University Press, 2005.

Esping-Andersen, Gøsta. *The Three Worlds of Welfare Capitalism.* Princeton, NJ: Princeton University Press, 1990.

Etzioni, Amitai. *The Spirit of Community: The Reinvention of American Society.* New York: Touchstone, 1993.

European Commission. *European Social Statistics: Migration.* Luxembourg: Office for Official Publications of the European Communities, 2002.

European Commission and the Council. *Joint Report by the Commission and the Council on Adequate and Sustainable Pensions.* Brussels: Council of the European Union, 2003.

Ferguson, Everett, ed. *Encyclopedia of Early Christianity.* New York: Garland, 1990.

Fisher, Gordon M. "The Development and History of the Poverty Thresholds." *Social Security Bulletin* 55, no. 4 (1992).

Frank, Thomas. *What's the Matter with Kansas?* New York: Henry Holt, 2004.

Freeman, Richard. *The Politics of Health in Europe.* Manchester: Manchester University Press, 2000.

Freud, Sigmund. *Civilization and Its Discontents.* Translated by Joan Riviere. New York: Jonathan Cape, 1930.

———. "Why War?" 1933. In *The Standard Edition of the Complete Psychological Works of Sigmund Freud*, vol. 22, edited and translated by James Strachey. London: Hogarth, 1964.

Fulton, Lionel. *Worker Representation in Europe.* Brussels: European Trade Union Institute, 2009.

Gauthier, Anne Hélène. *The State and the Family: A Comparative Analysis of Family Policies in Industrialized Countries.* Oxford: Clarendon Press, 1996.

Gerth, Hans H., and C. Wright Mills. *Character and Social Structure.* New York: Harcourt Brace, 1953.

Ghilarducci, Teresa. *When I'm Sixty-four: The Plot against Pensions and the Plan to Save Them*. Princeton, NJ: Princeton University Press, 2008.

Goldmann, Lucien. *The Human Sciences and Philosophy*. Translated by Hayden V. White and Robert Anchor. London: Jonathan Cape, 1969.

Graduate Institute of International and Development Studies. *Small Arms Survey, 2007*. Cambridge: Cambridge University Press, 2007.

Graduate Institute of International Studies, Geneva. *Small Arms Survey, 2003*. Oxford: Oxford University Press, 2003.

Hacker, Jacob S. *The Divided Welfare State: The Battle over Public and Private Social Benefits in the United States*. Cambridge: Cambridge University Press, 2002.

———. *The Great Risk Shift: The New Economic Insecurity and the Decline of the American Dream*. Rev. ed. New York: Oxford University Press, 2008.

Harrington, Michael. *The Other America*. New York: Macmillan, 1962.

Hartz, Louis. *The Liberal Tradition in America*. New York: Harcourt, Brace & World, 1955.

Hernando, Merino, and María Hernando. *Historia de los Inmigrantes Peruanos en España*. Madrid: Consejo Superior de Investigaciones Científicas, 2002.

Herzberg, Hendrik. "Like, Socialism." *New Yorker*, November 3, 2008.

Hobbes, Thomas. *Leviathan*. 1651. Cambridge: Cambridge University Press, 1991.

Institute of Medicine of the National Academies. *Insuring America's Health*. Washington, DC: National Academies Press, 2004.

Instituto Nacional de Estadística Geografía e Informática (INEGI). *XI Censo General de Población y Vivienda, 1990*. Aguascalientes: INEGI, 1992.

International Monetary Fund. *World Economic Outlook Update*, January 26, 2010.

Jaspers, Karl. *Nietzsche: An Introduction to the Understanding of His Philosophical Activity*. 1935. Translated by Charles F. Wallraff and Frederick J. Schmitz. Tucson: University of Arizona Press, 1965.

Jesuit, David, and Timothy Smeeting. "Poverty Levels in the Developed World." Luxembourg Working Paper No. 321, 2002. www.lisproject.org.

Julius, Deanne. "U.S. Economic Power: Waxing or Waning?" *Harvard International Review* 26, no. 4 (Winter 2005).

Kamerman, Sheila B., and Shirley Gatenio. "Tax Day: How Do America's Child Benefits Compare?" The Clearinghouse on International Developments in Child, Youth and Family Policies Issue Brief, Spring 2002.

Kaufmann, Walter. *Nietzsche: Philosopher, Psychologist, Antichrist*. 1950. Princeton, NJ: Princeton University Press, 1974.

Keynes, John Maynard. *The General Theory of Employment, Interest and Money*. New York: Harcourt Brace, 1936.

Kolchin, Peter. *American Slavery: 1619–1877*. New York: Hill and Wang, 1993.

Leisering, Lutz. "Germany: Reform from Within." In *International Social Policy*, edited by Pete Alcock and Gary Craig. Hampshire, UK: Palgrave, 2001.

"Let Market Dictate Wages." Editorial. *Hartford Courant*, February 18, 2004.

Lipset, Seymour Martin. *American Exceptionalism: A Double-Edged Sword*. New York: W. W. Norton, 1996.

Lipset, Seymour Martin, and Noah M. Meltz. *The Paradox of American Unionism*. Ithaca, NY: ILR Press of Cornell University Press, 2004.

Locke, John. *An Essay Concerning Human Understanding.* 1690. Edited by Peter H. Nidditch. Oxford: Oxford University Press, 1979.

———. *Two Treatises of Government.* 1690. Edited by Peter Laslett. Cambridge: Cambridge University Press, 1988.

Lohr, Steve. "Is Kaiser the Future of American Health Care?" *New York Times,* October 31, 2004, sec. 3, 1.

López, Luís Matías. "La Cuarta Edad: El gobierno quiere convertir la atención a las personas dependientes, ancianos en su mayoría, en el cuarto pilar del estado de bienestar." *El País* (Madrid), July 25, 2004, Domingo section, 1.

Luxembourg Income Study. "Key Figures Income Inequality Measures Table." www.lisproject.org/keyfigures/ineqtable.htm.

Mann, Thomas. *Confessions of Felix Krull—Confidence Man.* New York: Modern Library, 1965.

Mannheim, Karl. *Ideology and Utopia.* Translated by Louis Wirth and Edward Shils. New York: Harcourt, Brace & World, 1936.

Marcuse, Herbert. *Eros and Civilization.* 1955. Boston: Beacon, 1966.

Marx, Karl. *Capital.* Vol. 1. Translated by Samuel Moore and Edward Aveling. 1867. Moscow: Progress Publishers, n.d.

———. "Critique of the Gotha Programme." 1875. In *Karl Marx and Frederick Engels, Selected Works in Three Volumes.* Moscow: Progress Publishers, 1970.

———. *Economic and Philosophic Manuscripts of 1844.* Translated by Martin Mulligan. Moscow: Progress Publishers, 1959.

———. *Grundrisse.* 1857–1858. Translated by Martin Nicholas. Middlesex, UK: Penguin, 1973.

Mass, Bonnie. *Population Target: The Political Economy of Population Control in Latin America.* Brampton, ON: Charters, 1976.

Mazower, Mark. *Dark Continent: Europe's Twentieth Century.* New York: Vintage, 1998.

McDonnell, Ken. "Benefit Cost Comparisons between State and Local Governments and Private-Sector Employers." *EBRI [Employee Benefit Research Institute] Notes* 26, no. 4 (April 2005).

Mendes, Elizabeth. "Percentage of Uninsured Adults in U.S. Remains Elevated." *Gallup Poll,* March 17, 2010. www.gallup.com/poll/126791/Percentage -Uninsured-Adults-Remains-Elevated.aspx (accessed March 17, 2010).

Meyers, Marcia K., and Janet C. Gornick. "Early Childhood Education and Care (ECEC): Cross-National Variation in Service Organization and Financing." In *Early Childhood Education and Care: International Perspectives,* edited by Sheila B. Kamerman. New York: The Institute for Child and Family Policy at Columbia University, 2001. Testimony prepared for the United States Senate Committee on Health, Education, Labor, and Pensions, March 27, 2001.

Miles, Margaret R. "Augustine." In *Encyclopedia of Early Christianity,* edited by Everett Ferguson. New York: Garland, 1990.

Montagut, Teresa. *Política Social: Una Introducción.* Barcelona: Editorial Ariel, 2000.

Navarro, Vicente. "Luces y sombras de la reforma sanitaria de Obama." *Rebelión,* March 27, 2010. www.rebelion.org.

Nietzsche, Friedrich. *The Will to Power.* Translated by Walter Kaufmann and R. J. Hollingdale. 1901. New York: Random House, 1967.

Offe, Claus. *Contradictions of the Welfare State.* Edited by John Keane. Cambridge, MA: MIT Press, 1984.

Organization for Economic Cooperation and Development (OECD). *Benefits and Wages.* Paris: OECD, 2004.

———. *Benefit Systems and Work Incentives.* Paris: OECD, 1998.

———. *Education at a Glance 2009.* www.oecd.org/document/24/0,3343 ,en_2649_39263238_43586328_1_1_1_1,00.html (accessed April 7, 2010).

———. *Employment Outlook 2009.* Paris: OECD, 2009.

———. *Government at a Glance 2009.* www.oecd.org/document/33/0,3343 ,en_2649_33735_43714657_1_1_1_1,00.html#es (accessed March 31, 2010).

———. *Growing Unequal? Income Distribution and Poverty in OECD Countries.* Paris: OECD, 2008.

———. "Harmonised Unemployment Rates News Release: January 2010." www .oecd.org/dataoecd/20/21/44746304.pdf (accessed March 3, 2010).

———. *Health Data 2005.* Paris: OECD, 2005.

———. *Health Data 2009.* Paris: OECD, 2009.

———. *Measuring Public Employment in OECD Countries.* Paris: OECD, 1997.

———. *Pensions at a Glance: Retirement-Income Systems in OECD Countries.* Paris: OECD, 2009.

———. Social Expenditures Database. www.oecd.org/els/social/expenditure.

———. *Trade Union Density in OECD Countries, 1960–2007.* www.oecd.org/data oecd/25/42/39891561.xls (accessed March 31, 2010).

———. *Strukturprobleme des kapitalistischen Staates.* Frankfurt: Suhrkamp, 1972.

Orshansky, Mollie. "Children of the Poor." *Social Security Bulletin* 26, no. 7 (July 1963).

Padilla, Margarita Garcia. "Historia de la Acción Social: Seguridad Social y Asistencia (1939–1975)." In *Historia de la acción social pública en España: Beneficia y Previsión.* Madrid: Ministerio de Trabajo y Seguridad Social, 1990.

Peterson, Chris L., and Rachel Burton. "U.S. Health Care Spending: Comparison with Other OECD Countries." *Congressional Research Service,* September 17, 2007.

Pierson, Paul. *Dismantling the Welfare State? Reagan, Thatcher, and the Politics of Retrenchment.* Cambridge: Cambridge University Press, 1994.

Piven, Frances Fox. "Welfare and the Transformation of Electoral Politics." In *Social Policy and the Conservative Agenda,* edited by Clarence Y. H. Lo and Michael Schwartz. Malden, MA: Blackwell Publishers, 1998.

Piven, Frances Fox, and Richard A. Cloward. *Regulating the Poor: The Functions of Public Welfare.* 1971. New York: Vintage, 1993.

Polanyi, Karl. *The Great Transformation.* 1944. Boston: Beacon Press, 1957.

Proctor, Bernadette D., and Joseph Dalaker. Current Population Reports, P60–222, *Poverty in the United States: 2002.* Washington, DC: U.S. Government Printing Office, 2003.

Quadagno, Jill. "Social Security Policy and the Entitlement Debate: The New American Exceptionalism." In *Social Policy and the Conservative Agenda,* edited by Clarence Y. H. Lo and Michael Schwartz. Malden, MA: Blackwell Publishers, 1998.

Rampell, Catherine, and Matthew Saltmarsh. "A Reluctance to Retire Means Fewer Openings." *New York Times*, September 2, 2009.

Ray, Rebecca, Janet C. Gornick, and John Schmitt. "Parental Leave Policies in 21 Countries Assessing Generosity and Gender Equality." Washington, DC: Center for Economic and Policy Research, 2008.

Reich, Wilhelm. "Dialectical Materialism and Psychoanalysis." *Studies on the Left*, July–August 1966. Original publication in German in 1929.

Reinhardt, Uwe E., Peter S. Hussey, and Gerard F. Anderson. "Cross-National Comparisons of Health Systems Using OECD Data, 1999." *Health Affairs* 21, no. 3 (2002): 169–181.

Rifkin, Jeremy. *The European Dream: How Europe's Vision of the Future Is Quietly Eclipsing the American Dream*. New York: Jeremy P. Tarcher/Penguin, 2004.

Rousseau, Jean-Jacques. *Discourse on the Origin of Inequality*. 1755. Translated by Donald A. Cress. Indianapolis, IN: Hackett Publishing, 1992.

———. *The Social Contract*. 1762. Translated by G. D. H. Cole. New York: Hafner, 1951.

Russell, James W. *After the Fifth Sun: Class and Race in North America*. Englewood Cliffs, NJ: Prentice Hall, 1994.

———. *Class and Race Formation in North America*. Toronto: University of Toronto Press, 2009.

Sainsbury, Diane, and Ann Morissens. "European Anti-Poverty Policies in the 1990s: Toward a Common Safety Net?" Luxembourg Income Study Working Papers No. 307, 2002.

Sen, Amartya. *Development as Freedom*. New York: Anchor, 2000.

———. *Inequality Reexamined*. Cambridge, MA: Harvard University Press, 1992.

Skocpol, Theda. *Protecting Soldiers and Mothers: The Political Origins of Social Policy in the United States*. Cambridge, MA: Harvard University Press, 1992.

Smeeding, Timothy M. "Changing Income Inequality in OECD Countries: Updated Results from the Luxembourg Income Study." Luxembourg Income Study Working Papers No. 252, 2000.

———. "Poor People in Rich Nations: The United States in Comparative Perspective." Luxembourg Income Study Working Papers 419, October 2005.

———. "Public Policy, Economic Inequality, and Poverty: The United States in Comparative Perspective." *Social Science Quarterly* 86, no. 5 (December 2005).

Smith, Adam. *The Wealth of Nations*. 1776. Harmondsworth, UK: Penguin, 1982.

Smith, Kristin, Barbara Downs, and Martin O'Connell. "Maternity Leave and Employment Patterns." Current Population Reports, P70–79. Washington, DC: U.S. Census Bureau, November 2001.

Smith, Tom W. *2001 National Gun Policy Survey of the National Opinion Research Center: Research Findings*. Chicago: National Opinion Research Center, 2001.

———. *Public Attitudes toward the Regulation of Firearms*. Chicago: National Opinion Research Center, 2007.

Smith, William. *A Dictionary of Greek and Roman Antiquities*. London: John Murray, 1875.

Stark, Rodney. *The Rise of Christianity*. Princeton, NJ: Princeton University Press, 1996.

Stefansson, Claes-Goran. "Long-Term Unemployment and Mortality in Sweden, 1980–1986." *Social Science and Medicine* 32, no. 4 (1991): 419–23.

Tocqueville, Alexis de. *Democracy in America*. 1835. Translated by Henry Reeve. New York: Bantam, 2000.

United Nations Development Programme. *Human Development Report 2005*. New York: Oxford University Press, 2005.

———. *Human Development Report 2007/2008*. New York: Palgrave Macmillan, 2008.

United Nations Office on Drugs and Crime. "Seventh United Nations Survey of Crime Trends and Operations of Criminal Justice Systems, Covering the Period 1998–2000." www.unodc.org.

———. "Tenth Crime Trends Survey, 2005–2006."

U.S. Bureau of Justice Statistics. "Prisoners in 2008." http://bjs.ojp.usdoj.gov/index.cfm?ty=pbdetail&iid=1763 (accessed April 12, 2010).

U.S. Bureau of Labor Statistics. "Employer Costs for Employee Compensation Summary." News release, March 10, 2010. www.bls.gov/news.release/pdf/ecec.pdf (accessed April 1, 2010).

U.S. Bureau of the Census. *Statistical Abstract of the United States 2009*. Washington, DC: U.S. Government Printing Office, 2009.

———. *Statistical Abstract of the United States 2010*. Washington, DC: U.S. Government Printing Office, 2010. Table 648.

U.S. Department of Health and Human Services. "The 2009 HHS Poverty Guidelines." http://aspe.hhs.gov/poverty/09poverty.shtml (accessed April 3, 2010).

U.S. Department of Justice. "Prison and Jail Inmates at Midyear 2004." *Bureau of Justice Statistics Bulletin*, April 2005.

Van Hook, Jennifer, and Frank D. Bean. "Estimating Unauthorized Mexican Migration to the United States: Issues and Results." In U.S. Commission on Immigration Reform, *The Binational Study of Migration Between Mexico and the United States*, vol. 2 (1997).

Van Kersbergen, Kees. *Social Capitalism: A Study of Christian Democracy and the Welfare State*. London: Routledge, 1995.

Wagman, Daniel. "Integración y Inmigración." In *Inmigración y Seguridad*. Madrid: Edita Instituto Universitario de Investigaciones sobre Seguridad Interior, 2004.

Waldfogel, Jane. "Family and Medical Leave: Evidence from the 2000 Surveys." *Monthly Labor Review*, September 2001.

Walmsley, Roy. *World Prison Population List, 8th edition, International Centre for Prison Studies*. London: King's College, 2008.

Weber, Max. *Economy and Society*. 1922. New York: Bedminster Press, 1968.

———. *From Max Weber: Essays in Sociology*. Translated and edited by Hans H. Gerth and C. Wright Mills. New York: Oxford University Press, 1958.

———. *General Economic History*. Translated by Frank H. Knight. New York: Dover, 2003.

———. *The Protestant Ethic and the Spirit of Capitalism*. 1905. Translated by Talcott Parsons. London: Routledge, 1992.

Wodak, Ruth, and Maria Sedlak. "'We Demand that the Foreigners Adapt to Our Life Style': Political Discourse on Immigration Laws in Austria and the United Kingdom." In *Combating Racial Discrimination: Affirmative Action as a Model for Europe*, edited by Erna Appelt and Monika Jarosch. Oxford: Berg, 2000.

World Health Organization. *The World Health Report 2000*. Geneva: World Health Organization, 2000.

———. *The World Health Report 2005*. Geneva: World Health Organization, 2005.

Index

About the Author

James W. Russell is Connecticut State University Professor of Sociology at Eastern Connecticut State University. He has been a senior Fulbright Lecturer and Researcher in Mexico and the Czech Republic. He is the author of six books, including *Class and Race Formation in North America*, *Modes of Production in World History*, and *Societies and Social Life*.